Treating Infants and Young Children Impacted by Trauma

Concise Guides on Trauma Care Book Series

Child Maltreatment: A Developmental Psychopathology Approach
 Kathryn Becker-Blease and Patricia K. Kerig

*Treating Infants and Young Children Impacted by Trauma:
Interventions That Promote Healthy Development*
 Joy D. Osofsky, Phillip T. Stepka, and Lucy S. King

*Treating PTSD With Cognitive-Behavioral Therapies:
Interventions That Work*
 Candice M. Monson and Philippe Shnaider

Treating Infants and Young Children Impacted by Trauma

Interventions That Promote Healthy Development

Joy D. Osofsky, Phillip T. Stepka, and Lucy S. King

American Psychological Association • Washington, DC

Published by
American Psychological Association
750 First Street, NE
Washington, DC 20002
www.apa.org

To order
APA Order Department
P.O. Box 92984
Washington, DC 20090-2984
Tel: (800) 374-2721; Direct: (202) 336-5510
Fax: (202) 336-5502; TDD/TTY: (202) 336-6123
Online: www.apa.org/pubs/books
E-mail: order@apa.org

In the U.K., Europe, Africa, and the Middle East, copies may be ordered from
American Psychological Association
3 Henrietta Street
Covent Garden, London
WC2E 8LU England

Typeset in Minion by Circle Graphics, Inc., Columbia, MD

Printer: Edwards Brothers, Inc., Ann Arbor, MI
Cover Designer: Mercury Publishing Services, Inc., Rockville, MD

The opinions and statements published are the responsibility of the authors, and such opinions and statements do not necessarily represent the policies of the American Psychological Association.

Library of Congress Cataloging-in-Publication Data

Names: Osofsky, Joy D., author. | Stepka, Phillip T., author. | King, Lucy S., 1988- author.
Title: Treating infants and young children impacted by trauma : interventions that promote healthy development / Joy D. Osofsky, Phillip T. Stepka, and Lucy S. King.
Description: Washington, DC : American Psychological Association, [2017] | Series: Concise guides on trauma care book series | Includes bibliographical references and index.
Identifiers: LCCN 2016049294| ISBN 9781433827693 | ISBN 1433827697
Subjects: LCSH: Post-traumatic stress disorder in children—Treatment.
Classification: LCC RJ506.P55 O86 2017 | DDC 618.92/85210651—dc23 LC record available at https://lccn.loc.gov/2016049294

British Library Cataloguing-in-Publication Data
A CIP record is available from the British Library.

Printed in the United States of America
First Edition

http://dx.doi.org/10.1037/0000030-000

Contents

Series Foreword   *vii*
Anne P. DePrince and Ann T. Chu

Acknowledgments   *ix*

Introduction: Recognizing the Impact of Trauma
         Exposure on Young Children   3

1.   The Impact of Early Trauma on Development   15

2.   Child–Parent Psychotherapy   41

3.   Attachment and Biobehavioral Catch-Up Intervention 61

4.   Parent–Child Interaction Therapy   75

5.   Considerations in Choosing a Treatment That Works   93

Afterword: Conclusions and Future Directions   109

Appendix: Key Points on the Impact of Early
         Trauma on Development   115

References   117

Index   139

About the Authors   147

Series Foreword

Exposure to traumatic events is all too common, increasing the risk for a range of significant mental problems, such as posttraumatic stress disorder and depression; physical health problems; negative health behaviors, such as smoking and excessive alcohol consumption; impaired social and occupational functioning; and overall lower quality of life. As mass traumas (e.g., September 11, military engagements in Iraq and Afghanistan, natural disasters such as Hurricane Katrina) have propelled trauma into a brighter public spotlight, the number of trauma survivors seeking services for mental health consequences will likely increase. Yet despite the far-ranging consequences of trauma and the high rates of exposure, relatively little emphasis is placed on trauma education in undergraduate and graduate training programs for mental health service providers in the United States. Calls for action have appeared in the American Psychological Association's journal *Psychological Trauma: Theory, Research, Practice, and Policy* with such articles as "The Need for Inclusion of Psychological Trauma in the Professional Curriculum: A Call to Action" by Christine A. Courtois and Steven N. Gold (2009) and "The Art and Science of Trauma-Focused Training and Education" by Anne P. DePrince and Elana Newman (2011). The lack of education in the assessment and treatment of trauma-related distress and associated clinical issues at undergraduate and graduate levels increases the urgency to develop effective trauma resources for students as well as postgraduate professionals.

This book series, Concise Guides on Trauma Care, addresses that urgent need by providing truly translational books that bring the best of trauma psychology science to mental health professions working in diverse settings. To do so, the series focuses on what we know (and do not know) about specific trauma topics, with attention to how trauma psychology science translates to diverse populations (diversity broadly defined, in terms of development, ethnicity, socioeconomic status, sexual orientation, and so forth).

This series represents one of many efforts undertaken by Division 56 (Trauma Psychology) of the American Psychological Association to advance trauma training and education (e.g., see http://www.apatraumadivision. org/495/resource-directory.html). We are pleased to work with Division 56 and a volunteer editorial board to develop this series, which continues with the publication of this important book on treatments for infants and young children affected by trauma by Joy D. Osofsky, Phillip T. Stepka, and Lucy S. King. This book offers a practical and accessible overview of trauma-based treatments for children from birth through age 5. Bringing the best of developmental, clinical, and trauma psychological science perspectives to this book, Osofsky, Stepka, and King integrate essential information that will be of great use to mental health professionals serving young children who have been maltreated, neglected, or exposed to domestic violence and other traumatic events. Future books in the series will continue to build on these topics to address a range of assessment, treatment, and developmental issues in trauma-informed care.

Anne P. DePrince
Ann T. Chu
Series Editors

Acknowledgments

First, I (Joy D. Osofsky) want to thank my coauthors, Phillip T. Stepka and Lucy S. King, who have made the experience of writing this book both interesting and enjoyable as we shared ideas and developed a volume that we hope will not only be helpful to clinicians but also make a difference in the lives of young traumatized children. I am grateful to the faculty and trainees and the families who participate in the Louisiana State University Health Sciences Center's Harris Center for Infant Mental Health in the Department of Psychiatry for providing me with the opportunity to both teach and learn about traumatized young children and their families and ways to help them heal from their traumatic experiences. We all want to express appreciation to several of our professional colleagues for their incredible work and efforts in developing and working to disseminate the evidence-based treatments described in this book: Drs. Alicia Lieberman, Patricia Van Horn, and Chandra Ghosh Ippen for their knowledge and insights about child–parent psychotherapy; Drs. Robin Gurwitch of Duke University and Anthony Urquiza of the University of California, Davis, for their generous guidance regarding the application of parent–child interaction therapy to children exposed to trauma; and Dr. Mary Dozier for her creativity and advice related to the application of the attachment and biobehavioral catch-up intervention.

We also want to thank series editors Anne DePrince and Ann Chu and our development editor at the American Psychological Association,

David Becker, for their creativity in recognizing the importance of developing a publication related to young children exposed to trauma and encouraging us to write this important book. Their invaluable guidance helped us find the best ways to communicate this important information as clearly as possible to achieve our goals of informing readers about how to help young traumatized children and their families.

Finally, I want to thank my family. My husband, Howard, my loving partner and best friend, has consistently supported both my professional growth and enjoyment of family life and parenthood. My three children, Hari, Justin, and Michael, have provided me with the wonderful experience of what it means to have a family in which each is recognized and encouraged to grow and find his or her own way, which includes responsibility and caring for others. Now as adults, with very special spouses and children of their own, they have given me the joys of grandparenthood. I am very grateful to my family for consistently encouraging my efforts to help young children, especially those whose lives are affected by trauma and violence exposure.

Phillip T. Stepka would like to dedicate his efforts in writing this book to his son, Jackson. Despite having to adjust to Dad running the show while Mom was away at medical school, Jackson managed to muster enough resiliency not only to survive the creation of this book but also to keep their house full of sanity, smiles, and laughter throughout the process.

Lucy S. King would like to thank her academic mentors, Mary Ann Foley, Michelle Bosquet Enlow, Joy Osofsky, and Ian Gotlib, who have taught her to pursue her studies with integrity, persistence, and delight. Their consistent encouragement has been invaluable to both her personal and academic development.

Treating Infants and Young Children Impacted by Trauma

Introduction:
Recognizing the Impact of Trauma Exposure on Young Children

R esearch evidence, in addition to anecdotal information, indicates that children are exposed to a wide range of traumatic experiences during infancy and early childhood, a sensitive period for development (Osofsky, 2011). Indeed, in a representative sample of approximately 1,000 young children, Briggs-Gowan and colleagues (2010) found that by 2 to 3 years of age, approximately 26% of children had been exposed to trauma and 14% exposed to violence. Highlighting the vulnerability of particular groups, exposure was even more pronounced in children with additional risk factors. For example, 49% of children living in poverty had been exposed to trauma and were 2 to 5 times more likely to be exposed to violence. Researchers have documented a dose–response effect of childhood exposure to trauma, such that cumulative trauma places children at higher risk for long-term problems. Specifically, findings from the landmark Adverse Childhood Experiences Study (Felitti & Anda, 2010), which we describe

http://dx.doi.org/10.1037/0000030-001
Treating Infants and Young Children Impacted by Trauma: Interventions That Promote Healthy Development, by J. D. Osofsky, P. T. Stepka, and L. S. King

in more detail later, indicate that greater numbers of adverse experiences (e.g., domestic violence, abuse, neglect) are associated with greater risk of physical and mental problems in adulthood (e.g., depression, anxiety, heart disease). The study demonstrated the enormous societal cost of exposure to trauma in early life. Those individuals with greater numbers of adverse childhood experiences were also more likely to experience social problems, such as unemployment, family violence, parenting problems, and criminal behavior, with a higher use of health and social services.

These findings highlight the critical need for psychology and other health disciplines to devote greater attention to the effects of trauma on infant and early childhood mental health. Trauma, either recognized or unrecognized, is a major factor contributing to mental health symptoms in young children. I (Joy D. Osofsky) was instrumental in the development of the Harris Center for Infant Mental Health in 1996, an early effort to draw greater attention to the effects of early childhood trauma. With a grant from the Irving Harris Foundation, the Harris Center was established in the Department of Psychiatry at Louisiana State University Health Sciences Center to improve training in infant mental health and the implementation of evidence-based practices and services (Osofsky, Drell, Osofsky, Hansel, & Williams, 2016).

One of the first referrals to the Harris Center was twin boys aged 2 years and 11 months who had witnessed their mother's shooting death by their father 7 months earlier (Osofsky, Cohen, & Drell, 1995). We received the referral of these young children when they came from another state to live with their maternal grandparents. Other agencies stated they did not know how they could help these very young children with extreme symptoms. Although they were cute, their behavior was extremely dysregulated, and they only spoke a few words, which were difficult to understand. In our work with them, we learned firsthand about how extreme trauma exposure can lead to "freezing," "dissociation," and the inability to focus in young children. Although at that time questions were raised about whether it was possible to diagnose posttraumatic stress disorder in such young children, the two boys demonstrated diagnostic features, including repetitive, driven play, reexperiencing of the trauma set off by "trauma triggers" such as the color red (in Play-Doh), and avoidance and dissociation when they encountered play objects and subjects related to their mother. We were able to help these little boys and their grandparents with intensive treatment, assisting them to "get back on track" and return to a normal developmental trajectory. In turn, these little boys helped us in defining efforts to assist traumatized young children and their families. That experience 2 decades ago has profoundly influenced our efforts and commitment to helping very young children exposed to trauma and to making a difference in their lives.

We have used our experience over the years to help dispel the myth that infants and toddlers are not affected by trauma and to help promote understanding that early intervention and treatment can make a difference. An important part of our efforts has been the education of psychologists, psychiatrists, pediatricians, social workers, and other health professionals about the impact of trauma on young children and the evidence-based treatments that work. Clinicians have to learn about ways to understand young children, including their ways of telling us how they feel, especially when they are too young to communicate using language. Play has always been an important means by which young children communicate, with some authors even saying that "play is the language of children" (Landreth, 1983, p. 202). Further, clinicians must learn the importance of behavioral observations, through which we can learn how young children feel. Young children affected by trauma commonly show strong emotions; their reactions are most often expressed in dysregulated, typically aggressive or withdrawn behaviors.

To address these problems, the overall goals of this volume are two-fold. First, we provide the reader with a comprehensive understanding of the effects of different types of trauma on young children's development. Second, we use this understanding as a foundation for describing evaluations and "treatments that work" to address the effects of trauma on young children. Coordinated trauma-informed systems of care are needed to address the significant public health issue of early life stress and trauma. A trauma-informed system not only recognizes the effects of trauma on children and families but also works to establish policies and procedures that do not inadvertently retraumatize children at the same time as efforts are instituted to keep children safe (Howard & Tener, 2008; Ko et al., 2008).

The National Child Traumatic Stress Network (NCTSN), which has placed much emphasis on creating and supporting trauma-informed child and adult service systems, describes the importance of providing knowledge to help service providers and other individuals recognize and respond to the impact of traumatic exposure on young children and families whom they care for and serve. Within these systems, trauma awareness, knowledge, and skills can become part of the organizational culture, practices, and policies affecting all individuals who are involved with the child. Being trauma-informed also means using the best available science to support the recovery and resilience of the child.

NCTSN has proposed guidelines for mental health providers and child-serving services systems when incorporating trauma-informed practices that include (a) routine screening for trauma exposure and related symptoms; (b) using culturally appropriate evidence-based assessment and treatment for traumatic stress and associated mental health symptoms; (c) making resources available to children, families, and providers on trauma exposure, its impact, and treatment; (d) engaging in efforts to strengthen the resilience and protective factors of children and families affected by and vulnerable to trauma; (e) addressing parent and caregiver trauma and its impact on the family system; (f) emphasizing continuity of care and collaboration across child-service systems; and (g) maintaining an environment of care for staff that both addresses, minimizes, and treats secondary traumatic stress and also increases staff resilience. It is important for child service systems to receive training and consultation to develop and adhere to these important trauma-informed guidelines.

THE IMPORTANCE OF
THE PARENT–CHILD RELATIONSHIP

Readers of this book will gain an understanding of the importance of the parent–child relationship in supporting infants and young children who are exposed to traumatic events. Because young children have a more limited understanding and ability to cope with trauma than do older children, their sense of security comes from experiences in trusting, nurturing relationships with parents or adult caregivers who are available to understand their behavior and protect them, providing physical and emotional safety (Bowlby, 1988).

When young children experience trauma, their developing ability to maintain trust in relationships is threatened; if they are the target of or witness to violence by those whom they depend on for protection, it can not only dysregulate emotions and behaviors but also affect their view of themselves and others. For example, it is not unusual for a young child with a father who is a perpetrator of domestic violence and is in jail to react by becoming more active and anxious while also expressing that he misses his daddy. If adults describe his father as "bad," with the child's experience of his father as being important in his life, it can be confusing. With exposure to trauma and chronic stress, young children may begin to anticipate that they will have repeated negative experiences and may even think they are at fault. For children in the child welfare system, these negative perceptions can accompany them even when they are placed in a home that provides loving, nurturing relationships. For these reasons, sensitive relationship-based therapy can be helpful in working to modify these negative perceptions.

Parents can also be traumatized by similar violence exposure, such as domestic violence, which may make it more difficult for them to be emotionally available and supportive of their children. Common reactions in infants and toddlers include regression to earlier behaviors with more crying, clinging and fears of separation, aggression, and sleep or feeding problems. Preschool children exposed to trauma may lack self-confidence and be aggressive, anxious, and fearful. They may act out in social situations, have difficulty separating, imitate the behavior they have experienced or witnessed, complain of stomachaches or headaches, and show increased fear when an adult perpetrator is present. Exposure to trauma can also interfere with development, particularly social and emotional development. For all of these reasons, it is important to work together with both the young child and the parent to address the ongoing and sometimes shared traumatic experiences of both members of the dyad, including the past experiences of the parent that may be contributing to current difficulties.

THE IMPORTANCE OF UNDERSTANDING CUMULATIVE TRAUMATIC EXPERIENCES

The Adverse Childhood Experiences Study

The Adverse Childhood Experiences (ACE) Study carried out at Kaiser Permanente, with approximately 18,000 participants, is the largest study of its kind ever done to examine the effects of stress and trauma on well-being over the lifespan (Felitti et al., 1998). Although the ACE Study was retrospective (i.e., adults were interviewed about their past experiences), the findings provided foundational support for a cumulative risk model of the impact of early stress and trauma on well-being.

It is crucial to recognize that risk of negative outcomes increases markedly depending on the number of adverse early childhood experiences. Young children exposed to psychological, physical, or sexual maltreatment and those who come from dysfunctional households with domestic violence, substance abuse, or mental illness are more likely to experience negative outcomes because of exposure to significant, often multiple, adverse experiences with little support to buffer them from the effects. Young children with multiple adverse early experiences are more likely to demonstrate neurobiological effects, including brain abnormalities and dysregulation of biological stress response systems, as well as psychosocial effects. These effects may change in manifestation and intensity over time. In the school-age years, social problems and poor self-efficacy may become evident. As trauma-exposed children enter the adolescent years, they are more likely to participate in increasingly risky behaviors that affect their health and social environment, including smoking, overeating, lack of exercise, substance abuse, and promiscuity. Evidence-based prevention strategies, interventions, and treatments are critical for mitigating these negative outcomes. Such evidence-based treatments are described in Chapters 2, 3, and 4.

Since the original ACE Study, the ACE survey has been implemented with modifications for specific populations. The additional studies are helpful in broadening our understanding of the effects of early adverse experiences. The Philadelphia Urban ACE Study used the nine original ACE indicators—physical, sexual, or emotional abuse; physical or emotional neglect; witnessing domestic violence; living with someone who abused substances, was mentally ill, or imprisoned—and added five urban ACE indicators (Health Federation of Philadelphia, 2016)—experiencing racism, witnessing violence, living in an unsafe neighborhood, living in foster care, or experiencing bullying. The investigators included 1,784 Philadelphia residents throughout the city who were aged 18 years or older, representing a diverse range of socioeconomic, ethnic, and racial status. They were interviewed by telephone with a 67% response rate. When the authors compared their data with those of the Kaiser Permanente study, they found that the Philadelphia sample reported experiencing more emotional, physical, and sexual abuse and physical neglect. The authors concluded that individuals living in higher risk urban environments are likely to experience even more adverse childhood experiences that can have a negative impact on both their physical development and mental health.

In another relevant study, the San Francisco-based Center for Youth Wellness published *A Hidden Crisis* (C. Chen, 2014), which focused on 4 years (2008, 2009, 2011, 2013) of data collected from 27,745 adult residents of California. Health surveillance of these residents once again revealed physical, mental, and emotional health effects of traumatic childhood experiences. The authors concluded that to develop trauma-informed systems that can prevent early adversity and intervene more effectively among those exposed, it is important to screen young children for ACEs. Their data also suggested that instead of assuming there is "something wrong" with a young child who shows challenging behaviors and emotional dysregulation, it is also important to ask the child or caregivers "What happened to you?" The findings from these studies indicate an important direction for work related to trauma, which we further elaborate later in relation to developing trauma-informed child-serving systems.

Research on Polyvictimization

Exposure to interpersonal trauma, or trauma caused by other individuals, may have particularly detrimental effects. Finkelhor and colleagues (Finkelhor, Ormrod, & Turner, 2007; Finkelhor, Turner, Hamby, & Ormrod, 2011) conducted a series of population-based studies of children experiencing cumulative interpersonal trauma or, as they described it, *polyvictimization*. This research was conducted with a sample of over 2,000 children aged 2 to 17 years through telephone interviews with children or caregivers of the younger children. Surveys asked about child exposure to violence in the home and community—for example, physical assault, sexual assault, and burglary; child welfare violations such as child abuse, neglect, or family abduction; experience of warfare or civil disturbance; and bullying. The researchers found that a large proportion of the children who reported one type of victimization, such as sexual assault or bullying, reported a large number of additional types of victimization experienced during the prior year. In other words, multiple experiences of victimization are common when exposure to a single type is reported. Importantly, polyvictimization predicted trauma symptoms and had a greater influence on mental health than did single-type victimization. On the basis of these findings, Finkelhor and colleagues (2007, 2011) emphasized that to better understand negative experiences that lead to trauma symptoms, it is important to systematically study cumulative and interactive effects among different types of child victimization. Not only were victimized children more likely to experience additional victimization, they also had a higher level of additional lifetime adversities, including illnesses, accidents, family unemployment, parental substance abuse, and mental illness. The authors suggested that a more holistic approach to child victimization is needed to identify children who are at greatest risk of negative outcomes, with implications for treatment and public policy (Finkelhor et al., 2007, 2011).

OUTLINE OF THIS BOOK

In Chapter 1, we review research findings related to the effects of early trauma on psychobiological development, including the developing brain and physiology, cognitive and linguistic capacities, and emotions and relationships. Further, we highlight the effects of different types of trauma to which young children are exposed, with particular emphasis on maltreatment (abuse and neglect) and domestic violence.

In Chapters 2, 3, and 4, we describe three evidence-based treatments—child–parent psychotherapy, attachment and biobehavioral catch-up intervention, and parent–child interaction therapy—that are used in evaluating and providing services for young children affected by traumatic events. Each of these chapters describes the theoretical base, goals and evaluations, evidence base, and implementation strategies for these treatments. What is perhaps most important is for the reader to recognize that there are effective ways to intervene early, before a problem becomes increasingly difficult as the child grows older. All of the treatments are designed to support and restore not only the child, but also the caregiver–child relationship. An important message is that the caregiver and caregiving environment, as well as the child, are affected by trauma exposure.

Chapter 5 focuses on different treatment possibilities but also takes the reader a step further toward understanding what treatment works for whom (Fonagy et al., 2014). Here, we provide a road map to guide the reader through the criteria included in the evaluation process and the decision about which treatment might be most helpful for an individual child and caregiver. It is important that readers understand that the three treatments described in this book incorporate a developmental understanding of expected behavior in young children and integrate a sociocultural perspective related to background and beliefs in working with children and families. The Afterword provides a perspective on the fields of infant mental health and trauma and offers suggestions about directions for the future in these areas.

The overall goal of this volume is to help clinicians learn more about how to recognize and understand the effects of trauma exposure on young children, and evidence-based treatments that can make a difference in both the child's developmental trajectory and mental health. To raise awareness and increase knowledge in this area, infant mental health theory, research, and treatments should be included in training programs for all mental health professionals. Although infant mental health has recently been integrated into a number of training programs and clinical care settings, there are at present still a limited number that include infant mental health in their curriculum or have an infant and child track for psychology pre-doctoral internships, postdoctoral fellowships, or child psychiatry (Osofsky et al., 2016). Most programs still give little attention to training on evaluation and treatment of infants and young children. However, there is now abundant evidence not only about the need for, but also information about, evidence-based treatments that are effective for very young children, as indicated in a chapter in the *APA Handbook of Clinical Psychology* (Osofsky, 2016). Although other evidence-based treatments are helpful with older children exposed to trauma, such as trauma-focused cognitive behavioral therapy, the three treatments presented in this volume are specifically designed for use with children under the age of 6 years.

Early identification and treatment benefits from specialized training because the traumatic responses of infants and young children often are misinterpreted or misdiagnosed as developmental delays, difficult temperament, or behavior problems (ZERO TO THREE, 2005). Further, many clinicians who work with children have learned individual treatment approaches that focus on the child and parent separately. Although certainly appropriate in some cases, this treatment approach may not be optimal for infants and young children for whom the problems are best addressed within the context of the relationship. Because the burgeoning knowledge about brain development and the immediate and long-term impact of trauma in early life is rapidly advancing, this is an important time for psychologists and other mental health professionals to be trained in evidence-based treatments for young children affected by trauma. Further, the service gap is larger for minorities and families living in poverty, with significant disparities in care, and stress and trauma are also higher in these groups (Briggs-Gowan, Carter, & Ford, 2012; Shonkoff et al., 2012); therefore, training and technical assistance at all services levels are needed to close that gap. Psychologists have the opportunity to take the lead in increasing access to expert mental health care for children, including young children, exposed to trauma across developmental stages.

It has become clear in recent years that young children are often understood best in the context of their relationships. The quality of early development is important for later outcomes and, therefore, an understanding of early development is essential for addressing mental health issues and psychopathology in adults. Because we describe and elaborate on the problems that can develop early in life, readers will learn that early traumatic exposure can set a child on a path of developmental, behavioral, emotional, and mental health challenges. These challenges can be addressed or moderated by appropriate interventions, support, and treatment. Further, there is significant economic evidence that an educational and public health investment in prevention, intervention, and treatment will show large returns related to learning, productivity, and contributions to society (Knudsen, Heckman, Cameron, & Shonkoff, 2006).

We hope that readers of this book learn that early implementation of evidence-based treatments can prevent the negative effects of exposure to trauma, and significantly improve developmental outcomes for children.

The Impact of Early Trauma
on Development

The idea that our earliest experiences have lasting consequences for who we become has long been central to the field of psychology. It is perhaps surprising that many still believe that young children are not affected by early trauma, or if they are, they will naturally grow out of their negative reactions. Although many children demonstrate remarkable resilience in the face of adversity, a growing body of research indicates that although events that occur during the first years of life may feel distant or vague, their effects on biological, cognitive, and socioemotional development are significant.

In this chapter, we review research and theory describing how trauma in early life influences the development of young children. We provide information about how children's development can be altered, both adversely when children are exposed to trauma, and positively when children experience sensitive and responsive caregiving. This illustrative review provides

http://dx.doi.org/10.1037/0000030-002
Treating Infants and Young Children Impacted by Trauma: Interventions That Promote Healthy Development, by J. D. Osofsky, P. T. Stepka, and L. S. King

evidence that (a) although young children are exposed to a wide range of traumatic experiences, they are particularly vulnerable to maltreatment, including physical abuse, sexual abuse, and neglect; (b) disruptions due to trauma across multiple domains of development beget problems in later childhood, adolescence, and adulthood; (c) improving the quality of caregiving buffers children from the impact of trauma and promotes recovery; and (d) treatment for young children exposed to trauma should be initiated early and must target not only the child but also the caregiver and the caregiver–child relationship.

TYPES OF TRAUMA EXPOSURE IN YOUNG CHILDREN

As noted in the Introduction, exposure to trauma in early life is common, particularly among children living in poverty. As described next, young children are disproportionately exposed to maltreatment and domestic violence during the earliest years of life. Thus, we focus on these forms of trauma in this chapter.

Maltreatment

Although an important role of parents and other caregivers is to protect children from external stressors, they may, unfortunately, also serve as the source of trauma when they are abusive or neglectful. Indeed, much of the research on the consequences of trauma in early life has focused on exposure to maltreating caregivers. This research is driven by the theory that young children rely on behavioral cues from their caregivers for development (Bowlby, 1988) and that development is disturbed when caregivers do not provide adequate positive environmental input (e.g., prompt and sensitive responses to child distress and exploration) or instead deliver harmful input (e.g., verbal or physical harm; Humphreys & Zeanah, 2015).

Child maltreatment can be defined as behavior toward a child that is both outside the norms of social conduct and entails a substantial risk of causing physical or emotional harm. Using this definition, the recognized types of maltreatment include physical abuse, sexual abuse, emotional abuse, and neglect. The causes of child maltreatment are varied and often relate to intergenerational experiences of maltreatment and parental factors, such as substance abuse and mental illness (Appleyard, Berlin, Rosanbalm, & Dodge, 2011). As shown in Figure 1.1, young children are at pronounced risk of experiencing maltreatment. According to the U.S. Department of Health and Human Services (DHHS), 3.5 million reports of child maltreatment were made to Child Protective Services (CPS) in 2013, involving 6.4 million children (Child Welfare Information Gateway, 2015). Sixty-one percent (1.1 million) of these reports were investigated in detail, and about 679,000 maltreated children were identified. Although boys and girls were exposed equally to maltreatment, younger children had higher rates of victimization. Indeed, as depicted in Figure 1.1, children in the first year of life had the highest rate of victimization. Moreover, 81% of fatalities due to maltreatment were children 0 to 3 years old.

Among children exposed to maltreatment, over 75% are neglected (Child Welfare Information Gateway, 2015). In addition to the failure

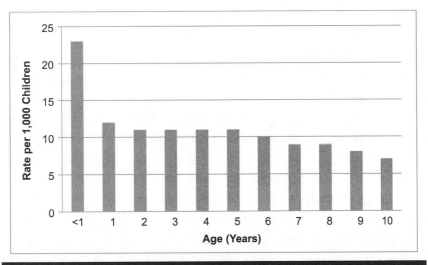

Figure 1.1

Exposure to maltreatment by age. Adapted from *Child Maltreatment 2013* (p. 22), by the U.S. Department of Health and Human Services, Administration for Children and Families, Administration on Children, Youth and Families, Children's Bureau, 2015. Retrieved from http://www.acf.hhs.gov/programs/cb/research-data-technology/statistics-research/child-maltreatment. In the public domain.

to meet a child's physical needs, neglect includes the failure to meet the socioemotional, medical, and/or educational needs of a child (Stoltenborgh, Bakermans-Kranenburg, & van IJzendoorn, 2013). As neglect often co-occurs with abuse, it has been difficult to identify its unique impact on child development. Indeed, researchers have noted that there has been a "neglect of child neglect" in research on maltreatment (Stoltenborgh et al., 2013, p. 1). In this chapter, however, we review important evidence from studies of children deprived of appropriate caregiving while living in orphanages. Although the generalizability of this evidence is somewhat limited (i.e., children neglected by their parents have different experiences), it clearly demonstrates that development depends on the fulfillment of both emotional and physical needs. Similarly, research on the impact of emotional abuse has demonstrated the importance of appropriate emotional input. This form of abuse is highly prevalent, with worldwide estimates that it affects 35% of children (Stoltenborgh, Bakermans-Kranenburg, Alink, & van IJzendoorn, 2012). Although emotional abuse is not grounds for investigation by CPS, research has shown that its impact on mental health is equally or more severe than that of physical abuse, sexual abuse, or neglect. In a recent study of over 2,000 ethnically diverse children in the United States, the harmful psychiatric and behavioral effects of emotional abuse were found to be equivalent to those of other forms of maltreatment (Vachon, Krueger, Rogosch, & Cicchetti, 2015).

One challenge facing both the research and implementation of treatment for abused and neglected young children is that these experiences often go unreported. About two thirds of all reports to CPS in 2013 were made by professionals who are mandated to report maltreatment (e.g., educators, law enforcement, day care providers, medical or mental health personnel; Child Welfare Information Gateway, 2015). This indicates that victims, parents, and other family members and friends are less likely to report child maltreatment. Young children, especially, lack the capacity to identify and verbalize their experiences, and children of all ages may fear retribution or feel ashamed, sometimes believing that what happened was their fault. Parents may also lack awareness that their behavior toward their child constitutes maltreatment and could be seriously harmful. For example, parents may not be aware of the importance of emotional availability and responsiveness. Others may be members of families and communities that, based on cultural mores, have endorsed corporal punishment of children; most will not know that research identifies associations between such physical discipline and child maladjustment (Lansford et al., 2014). In their 2013 report, DHHS stated that 18% of child maltreatment victims identified by CPS experienced physical abuse. As described in Chapter 3, interventions for maltreated children may focus on increasing parents' awareness of their behavior and how it affects their children.

Sexual abuse is a particularly stigmatized form of maltreatment and often goes unreported. Sexual abuse involves any sexual activity between a child and another person for which consent is either not given or not able to be given due to the developmental or intellectual capacity of the child (Berliner & Elliott, 2002). Recent data indicate that 9% of CPS cases involved sexual abuse in 2013 (Child Welfare Information Gateway, 2015), and it is estimated that one in seven of all sexually abused children are below the age of 6 years (Berliner & Elliott, 2002; Snyder, 2000). Frequently, sexual abuse, even when reported, is not substantiated on either medical or forensic examination. Young children exposed to sexual abuse may experience shame and self-blame. Not infrequently, they may develop a poor body image, regression, and sexualized behavior.

Domestic Violence

In addition to direct victimization through abuse, young children can be indirectly exposed to violence when they witness their parents or other family members engage in domestic violence. Such acts include verbal threats of violence, displaced aggression (e.g., breaking things, throwing things, punching walls), or physical assaults on adults or children (e.g., hitting, slapping, pushing, kicking, choking). According to a U.S. Department of Justice survey of approximately 4,500 children, 25% had been exposed to some form of domestic violence, with 17% of 0–5-year-olds exposed (Hamby, Finkelhor, Turner, & Ormrod, 2011). Similar to maltreatment, domestic violence may be particularly detrimental for young children because it involves caregivers, who are critical for early development and who are supposed to protect children (Bosquet Enlow, Blood, & Egeland, 2013). Children exposed to domestic violence do not learn appropriate, effective, and safe ways to express anger, which may lead to long-term aggressive behavior.

Because of their limited developmental capacities, young children are especially unable to cope with or regulate fearful responses. For example, although common child reactions to domestic violence include yelling at parents to stop, trying to get away, or calling for help (Hamby et al., 2011), young children are unable to react in these potentially constructive ways. Paired with the limited developmental capacity to respond is the young child's acute awareness of the interparental conflict. Far from being oblivious to domestic violence, even sleeping babies, especially babies exposed to high interparental conflict in their daily lives, show increased neural responses to angry voices (Graham, Fisher, & Pfeifer, 2013).

THE IMPACT OF TRAUMA ON THE DEVELOPING BRAIN AND PHYSIOLOGY

During the first years of life, biological development is rapid. In the brain of a healthy toddler, for example, synapses (i.e., neural connections) are formed at the peak rate of 2 million per second (ZERO TO THREE, 2012). According to the theory that the first years of life are a sensitive period, this state of plasticity renders young children particularly open to biological alterations by the environment, which may have cascading effects on subsequent biological, socioemotional, and cognitive functioning. Although experiences such as sensitive caregiving and cognitive stimulation can initiate a "broaden-and-build" cycle of long-term resilience and flourishing (Fredrickson, 2004), traumatic experiences can have enduring negative consequences (Shonkoff et al., 2012). In this section, we review theory and findings illustrating the impact of early trauma on the developing brain and physiology.

Trauma and Biological Reactivity and Regulation

Trauma in the first years of life appears to compromise the biological systems that govern how children respond to stress and fear, including (a) the hypothalamic–pituitary–adrenal (HPA) axis, (b) the autonomic nervous system, and (c) neural circuitry involving the amygdala and the prefrontal cortex. These systems control stress *reactivity*, defined by the speed and intensity of response to a stressor, as well as stress *regulation*, defined by the tendency to modulate or control this response. In the context of extremely frightening and overwhelming events, children can become biologically *dysregulated*, such that reactivity is aberrant and regulation is impaired. Importantly, biological dysregulation has been linked to a host of negative psychological and physical health outcomes, including depression (LeMoult, Chen, Foland-Ross, Burley, & Gotlib, 2015), anxiety (Dierckx et al., 2012), posttraumatic stress disorder (PTSD; Weems & Carrion, 2007), attention-deficit/hyperactivity disorder (ADHD; Isaksson, Nilsson, Nyberg, Hogmark, & Lindblad, 2012), and other behavior problems (Doom, Cicchetti, & Rogosch, 2014).

Trauma, the Hypothalamic–Pituitary–Adrenal Axis, and the Autonomic Nervous System

The HPA axis controls the release and regulation of the "stress hormone," cortisol, which typically increases in reaction to acute stress and then decreases after reaching its height. Although the HPA axis response is prolonged, with cortisol levels reaching their peak approximately 20 minutes following a stressor, the response of the autonomic nervous system (ANS) is immediate and can be understood as the body's fight-or-flight response, including sympathetic activity, which releases epinephrine and increases heart and respiration rates, and parasympathetic activity, which returns the body to rest. The flexibility of both the HPA axis and the ANS allows the body to maintain equilibrium by responding to stress and recovering from it efficiently (McEwen, Gray, & Nasca, 2015). Thus, moderate reactivity of the HPA axis and the ANS is important for adaptation.

According to the theory of *allostatic overload*, the wear and tear on biological reactivity and regulation systems due to chronic activation during the first years of life may ultimately result in their systemic failure and concomitant health problems (McEwen & Wingfield, 2003). Other theories, including that of *biological sensitivity to context* or *differential susceptibility*, suggest that children's outcomes depend on interactions between their innate tendency toward reactivity and the quality of their environment (Ellis, Boyce, Belsky, Bakermans-Kranenburg, & van IJzendoorn, 2011). Although findings have been mixed, blunted reactivity of the HPA axis, indicating the inability of this system to respond to stress, has been a commonly documented pattern in children exposed to abuse and neglect (Bruce, Fisher, Pears, & Levine, 2009; Cicchetti & Rogosch, 2001; Jaffee et al., 2015). Although blunting of the stress response may have short-term benefits for survival in the context of persistent trauma, it appears to have long-term costs for mental and physical health.

Through prospective, longitudinal studies of children raised in orphanages and foster care, mental health researchers have learned a great deal about the downstream consequences of early caregiving deprivation (i.e., neglect) and improvements in care on biological reactivity and regulation systems. Specifically, findings from the Bucharest Early Intervention Project (BEIP; Nelson, Fox, & Zeanah, 2014) indicate that children exposed to long-term institutionalization demonstrate a pervasive pattern of blunted HPA axis and ANS functioning in response to a series of psychosocial stressors (McLaughlin et al., 2015). The plasticity of human biology in early life increases the degree to which stress "gets under the skin," but it may also permit biological recovery following intervention. Indeed, McLaughlin and colleagues (2015) found that children who eventually received family-based care demonstrated patterns of functioning that more closely resembled children who were never institutionalized. These results point to causal effects of the early caregiving environment on the development of the HPA axis and ANS and indicate that early caregiving deprivation (i.e., neglect) has lasting consequences for stress responses. Interventions that improve the quality of care, however, can help normalize aberrant patterns of stress reactivity. Importantly, findings from the BEIP have led to significant policy changes in Romania, where institutionalization has since been banned for children under the age of 2 years (Nelson et al., 2014).[1]

---

[1] The BEIP was undertaken with intense oversight to protect vulnerable participants and with a policy of noninterference when it came to the placements of children in the study. Critically, if the local Commissions on Child Protection in Bucharest directed that children in either group could be adopted or returned to their families of origin, the research team did not interfere. The ethical issues of this project have been discussed at length elsewhere (Miller, 2009; Millum & Emanuel, 2007; Nelson, Fox, & Zeanah, 2014; Rid, 2012; Zeanah, Fox, & Nelson, 2012).

The powerful influence of early caregiving on the HPA axis has also been observed in research examining patterns of diurnal cortisol regulation. In addition to responding to acute stress, the HPA axis regulates the release of cortisol throughout the day. In typically developing individuals, cortisol follows a rhythm in which it peaks after awakening (i.e., the cortisol awakening response) and then gradually decreases, reaching its lowest levels at bedtime. As observed in research examining the cortisol response to acute stress, many studies examining diurnal cortisol indicate that early trauma is associated with a blunted pattern, such that there is a diminished increase in cortisol in the morning and a flat slope across the day. This pattern has been observed later in childhood as a downstream consequence of early trauma (Cicchetti & Rogosch, 2001; Kuhlman, Geiss, Vargas, & Lopez-Duran, 2015); it has also been identified in young children with histories of exposure to abuse or neglect. For example, Bernard, Zwerling, and Dozier (2015) found that children who had been maltreated in infancy showed a blunted pattern of diurnal cortisol by 3 to 6 years of age. In turn, this dysregulated pattern predicted greater externalizing symptoms.

Positive parental presence, however, appears to buffer children from chronic activation of stress response systems that may lead to atypical patterns of cortisol. For example, in a study of 6-month-old infants, Bosquet Enlow, King, and colleagues (2014) found that high maternal sensitivity during a parent–child stressor facilitated adaptive reactivity and regulation among infants, such that HPA axis and ANS responses increased in response to maternal withdrawal (the stressor) but returned to baseline on maternal reunion (the recovery). In contrast, infants of mothers low in sensitivity showed amplified reactivity to the stressor and failed to recover. Amplified reactivity among infants may precede the later emergence of blunted HPA axis and ANS responses (Gunnar & Quevedo, 2007). Positive caregiving may prevent this negative process.

Trauma, the Amygdala, and the Prefrontal Cortex

The benefits of positive parental presence for reactivity and regulation have also been observed in studies of neural responses to threat, including those of the amygdala and the prefrontal cortex (PFC). In the first years of life, the amygdala, a bilateral brain structure important for response to emotional stimuli, appears to be particularly reactive (Gee et al., 2013b). Simultaneously, the activity of the PFC, theorized to exert top-down regulatory control of emotional responses, is relatively attenuated. An "immature" childhood profile of amygdala–PFC coupling is hypothesized to explain early fears such as separation anxiety (Gee et al., 2013b). Like the HPA axis and the ANS, the plasticity of amygdala–PFC circuitry in the first years of life increases susceptibility to environmental influences.

If young children lack the profile of neural coupling important for regulating emotional reactivity, how do they learn to successfully recover from intense negative emotional states? Research indicates that during the sensitive period of early life, parental stimuli play a supplemental role in regulation by dampening the reactivity of the amygdala (Gee et al., 2014). Theoretically, through consistent parental presence, a pattern of reduced amygdala reactivity and enhanced PFC activity becomes entrained by adolescence, such that older individuals can navigate challenging emotional stimuli independently (Callaghan & Tottenham, 2016). As positive maternal presence appears to facilitate optimal coupling of the amygdala and PFC, a likely hypothesis is that early caregiving deprivation and neglect may lead to atypical development of amygdala–PFC circuitry.

There is empirical evidence that children who cannot depend on their caregivers to modulate amygdala reactivity in early life demonstrate differences in the development of neural circuitry. In a study of previously institutionalized children, Gee and colleagues (2013a) found that the development of amygdala–PFC circuitry was accelerated among previously institutionalized children, such that they showed a more mature profile of amygdala–PFC coupling. Despite the potentially compensatory effects of accelerated development, previously institutionalized children displayed heightened amygdala reactivity to fearful faces relative to a comparison group of children raised in family settings. Although not yet well understood, a premature shift to an adult-like coupling of brain regions among children exposed to early trauma may operate similarly to a blunting of HPA axis responses. Although early arrival at a mature profile may assist in immediate survival when activation of the amygdala is chronic, truncated development of amygdala–PFC circuitry may ultimately result in problematic functioning. Studies demonstrate that child maltreatment leaves "limbic scars," with adults who experienced maltreatment displaying hyperactivity of the amygdala in response to threat (Dannlowski et al., 2012) and aberrations in amygdala–PFC coupling (Jedd et al., 2015).

Trauma and Structural Brain Development

Although further research is needed to resolve discrepant findings (Humphreys & Zeanah, 2015), emerging work has indicated that trauma in early life may result in atypical development of brain structure. Perhaps the most dramatic findings come from studies of children exposed to extreme neglect and sensory deprivation, who have substantially smaller brain sizes (Perry & Pollard, 1997). Structural changes following early exposure to trauma have also been observed across several different regions of the brain (Teicher & Samson, 2016). Studies of adults exposed to childhood maltreatment (McCrory, De Brito, & Viding, 2010) and children and adolescents exposed to caregiving deprivation (Hodel et al., 2015) and parental psychopathology (M. C. Chen, Hamilton, & Gotlib, 2010) have revealed bilateral reductions in the volume of the hippocampus. Central to learning and memory, the hippocampus is also the primary site for glucocorticoid (cortisol) receptors in the brain and is thus highly susceptible to damage from atypical levels of cortisol. Assessing hippocampal volume in 3- to 6-year-old children, Luby and colleagues (2013) found that volume was smaller among children exposed to poverty and that this association was driven by hostile parenting and stressful life events. Pointing to the powerful effects of caregiving on brain development, Rifkin-Graboi et al. (2015) found that even normal variation in maternal sensitivity predicted infant hippocampal volume.

In addition to findings on hippocampal volume, studies of maltreated children and adolescents have identified atypical amygdala volume. Like the hippocampus, the amygdala has a high density of glucocorticoid receptors and therefore may be affected by aberrant levels of cortisol. In their recent review of the neurobiological effects of child maltreatment, Teicher and Samson (2016) noted that increases in amygdala volume have been identified among children and adolescents exposed to early emotional and/or physical neglect, including those deprived of care due to institutionalization (Mehta et al., 2009; Tottenham et al., 2010) and those exposed to chronic maternal depression (Lupien et al., 2011). In contrast, decreases in amygdala volume have been more often identified in older adolescents and adults exposed to multiple forms of maltreatment across development. Overall, it may be that early exposure to maltreatment drives an initial increase in amygdala volume, with further exposure resulting in reductions in volume that are observable only later in development.

Trauma-Induced Changes in Cellular Aging and Gene Expression

Emerging work using human and animal models indicates that trauma may also increase the risk of negative health outcomes through alterations in cellular aging and gene expression (Van den Bergh, 2011). In a process termed *epigenetic programming*, genes are silenced or switched on following exposure to trauma, such that the experience is in effect made permanent at the genetic level and influences future functioning. Markers of cellular aging and epigenetic changes following early trauma include shortening of DNA telomeres and anomalous DNA methylation in genes linked to stress and mental health.

Telomeres are the protective caps at the end of each strand of DNA. Their length is an index of biological aging such that shorter telomeres are associated with older age, higher risk of disease, and earlier death. Research has suggested that early trauma may lead to "telomere erosion"— children exposed to experiences such as maltreatment have shorter telomeres (Shalev et al., 2013). These findings indicate that young children are not only at increased risk of death from the direct physical insult of maltreatment but may also have shorter life expectancies after the direct experience of trauma has ceased. Perhaps most concerning, reduced telomere length has even been identified in young adults exposed to stress in utero, with estimates that this reduction in telomere length equates to an additional 3.5 years in cellular aging (Entringer et al., 2011). Although beyond the scope of this book, these findings accompany those of numerous other studies indicating that children of mothers exposed to stress and trauma in pregnancy show changes in biological markers of stress (Bock, Wainstock, Braun, & Segal, 2015).

Greater DNA methylation, associated with the silencing of gene expression, has been identified in children exposed to stress and trauma. In a longitudinal sample, Essex and colleagues (2013) found that children who had been exposed to high parental stress in the first year of life had greater methylation at age 15 across a large number of DNA sites, some of which had been previously linked to early familial stress and adversity. In another study of infants, researchers found that those exposed to prenatal maternal depression or anxiety had greater methylation in genes that regulate cortisol (Conradt, Lester, Appleton, Armstrong, & Marsit, 2013). Although unpacking gene–environment interactions requires further research, findings related to the epigenetic effects of stress exposure suggest a potential "fundamental cause" of atypical development and poor health outcomes (Essex et al., 2013, p. 71).

THE IMPACT OF TRAUMA ON COGNITIVE AND LINGUISTIC DEVELOPMENT

Simultaneous with rapid biological development in the first years of life, cognitive development advances dramatically. The steepest gains in executive function skills occur in a stepwise fashion between birth and age 6. These skills, including working memory, inhibitory control, attentional control, and cognitive flexibility, are the "building blocks" for learning and academic achievement (National Scientific Council on the Developing Child, 2011). Indeed, scientists cite executive function as more important for school readiness than specific knowledge of numbers or letters (National Scientific Council on the Developing Child, 2011), with working memory and attentional control predicting emergent literacy and numeracy skills in kindergarten (Welsh, Nix, Blair, Bierman, & Nelson, 2010). Closely tied to executive function, the development of language occurs at a rapid pace in the first years of life. Typically developing children say their first word at 13 months and form their first sentences less than a year later. By 5 or 6 years, they have learned the meaning of thousands of words, mastered the basic grammatical structure of language, and can engage in sustained conversations. With adult competence rooted in child and adolescent achievement, children who successfully acquire cognitive and linguistic skills in early life are equipped to flourish in the future (Masten & Tellegen, 2012).

Unfortunately, not all children follow a trajectory of healthy cognitive and linguistic development. Devastating early case studies such as that of Genie, who was severely neglected and abused from the age of 18 months to 13 years and emerged with pervasive motor and speech deficits (Curtiss, 1977), demonstrated the consequences of the most extreme forms of maltreatment. Since then, a large body of research has supported the hypothesis that early life is a sensitive period for cognitive and linguistic development. This research includes studies of the effects of familial risk factors (e.g., poverty) and suboptimal caregiving (e.g., insensitivity), as well as trauma (e.g., domestic violence), on cognition and language in young children.

Familial Risk, Suboptimal Caregiving, and Cognition and Language

Perhaps the most widely reported findings indicating that early life is a sensitive period for cognitive and linguistic development have been those identifying striking disparities in abilities between children who grow up in contexts of poverty compared with those who develop with more financial resources, which contribute to other advantages (Halle et al., 2009; Votruba-Drzal, Miller, & Coley, 2016). In their seminal study, *The Early Catastrophe*, Hart and Risley (2003) documented a 30-million word gap between children age 3 who lived in poverty and those who lived in affluence. For 2½ years, the authors observed 42 families for 1 hour each month, recording over 1,300 hours of casual interactions between parents and their language-learning children. They found that poor children heard one third the number of words per hour than more affluent children did. The quality of these words also differed along socioeconomic lines; the average child from an affluent family heard 166,000 encouragements and 26,000 discouragements per year, whereas the average child from a low-income family heard 26,000 encouragements and 57,000 discouragements. In a more recent study of language development during the first 2 years of life, Fernald, Marchman, and Weisleder (2013) found that toddlers of low socioeconomic status (SES) lagged 6 months behind their high SES counterparts in the processing skills (i.e., accuracy, speed) necessary for language.

Children in poverty may experience different forms of parenting and have caregivers who are exposed to greater levels of stress and trauma. Optimal cognitive development requires appropriate stimulation and scaffolding from caregivers. As a corollary, the environment must be one in which exploration is safe rather than scary, and caregivers must be perceived as sources of stimulation and help, rather than sources of threat. In addition to lacking the financial resources to furnish an environment with stimulating toys and books, caregivers under financial strain may live in more dangerous places and, due to higher daily stress, encounter greater challenges in engaging in the caregiving behaviors (e.g., establishing routines and talking to their children) that promote their children's cognitive development. Indeed, poverty is associated with higher rates of exposure to household and community violence, as well as an increased likelihood of unresponsive and harsh care, abuse, and neglect (Evans, 2004; Ondersma, 2002). Therefore, reductions in the number and quality of words poor children hear may be tied to exposure to trauma and suboptimal caregiving.

Both the direct actions of caregivers that support the acquisition of cognitive and linguistic capacities and the indirect effects of familial factors such as poverty and household functioning influence cognitive development. For example, *scaffolding* involves the direct, in-the-moment actions of caregivers that support child learning by modeling skills, narrating actions, and providing help when needed. In contrast, positive household functioning has an indirect effect on learning by providing the safe context in which beneficial interactions take place. To integrate information about the impact of both direct and indirect familial factors on development, Hughes and Ensor (2009) used multiple observational and self-report measures of family life and executive function among young children. When controlling for executive function at age 2, they found that executive function at age 4 was associated with caregiving behaviors such as greater maternal scaffolding and planning, as well as reduced chaos in the family context. Although greater scaffolding and planning predicted higher executive function, problematic household functioning predicted poorer executive function.

The results of Hughes and Ensor (2009) indicated that the effects of both familial risk factors and caregiving behaviors on development manifest quickly, revealing themselves in measurable changes in executive function between children's second and fourth birthdays. Familial risk factors may also co-occur in different ways across individuals, with various combinations exerting distinct effects. Using a person-centered approach, Rhoades, Greenberg, Lanza, and Blair (2011) identified six subgroups of children characterized by particular constellations of familial risk factors in infancy. These groups were defined by differences in the likelihood of living in poverty or a crowded household, as well as by having a mother who was single, smoked while pregnant, gave birth to her first child as a teenager, had mood problems, had greater life stress, or had low social support. The authors found that particular constellations of risk factors in infancy uniquely predicted executive function (working memory, inhibitory control, and cognitive flexibility) in toddlerhood. Among Caucasian children, membership in either of the subgroups defined by having a mother who was married (*mother married, low risk* or *mother married, stressed and depressed*) was associated with the best executive function outcomes. In contrast, among African American children, only membership in the lowest risk group (*mother married, low-risk*) was related to better executive function.

The findings of Rhoades and colleagues (2011) suggest that unique combinations of multiple familial factors may best capture variability in executive function outcomes. Importantly, they also provided information about an understudied process—that is, how familial risk factors operate differently across racial and ethnic groups. The next step would be to ask how these profiles of risk lead to problems with executive function in toddlerhood. In line with burgeoning research indicating the powerful effects of early caregiving on development, Rhoades et al. found that the quality of observed parenting behavior in infancy explained the association between familial risk in infancy and executive function in toddlerhood. Specifically, caregiving could either help or hinder young children exposed to familial risk. Greater maternal engagement conferred benefits whereas greater maternal intrusiveness led to more negative outcomes.

Trauma and Cognition and Language

Research among young traumatized children has indicated that domestic violence and maltreatment have negative consequences for cognition and language above and beyond those conferred by poverty. For example, after controlling for socioeconomic status, Eigsti and Cicchetti (2004) identified significant language delays among preschool children exposed to abuse and neglect in infancy. One mechanism for this association may be differences in the linguistic input provided by maltreating parents. Providing trauma-specific insight into the "early catastrophe" identified by Hart and Risley (2003), Eigsti and Cicchetti found that mothers of maltreated children spoke fewer words during parent–child interactions, asked fewer questions, produced less complex sentences, and used more negative imperatives. In a more recent study, Cowell, Cicchetti, Rogosch, and Toth (2015) found that the timing and severity of maltreatment were associated with deficits in executive function in children age 3 to 9 years. Specifically, children exposed to maltreatment during infancy and children exposed to chronic maltreatment exhibited significantly poorer inhibitory control and working-memory performance than did children with no history of maltreatment. As noted earlier, maltreatment during infancy may disrupt the development of brain structures and functions that support cognition and language, with continued exposure worsening these deficits.

Fewer studies have used longitudinal designs to examine the consequences of exposure to familial violence in early life on cognitive development in young children. Such research is important for identifying causal effects of early trauma and understanding how these effects cascade over time. In a sample of low-income mothers and children participating in the Minnesota Longitudinal Study of Parents and Children, Bosquet Enlow, Egeland, Blood, Wright, and Wright (2012) assessed child IQ, family sociodemographic variables, and exposure to intimate partner violence in repeated observational sessions and interviews across the first 5 years of life. Once again, earliest exposure to trauma appeared to have the most detrimental effects on child IQ, such that intimate partner violence exposure in infancy, but not in preschool only, was associated with poorer cognitive outcomes. Indeed, exposure to intimate partner violence in infancy predicted a 7.25-point lower child cognitive scores from 24 to 96 months of age after controlling for child birth weight, cognitive stimulation in the home, and maternal age, education, and SES. In influential work describing the policy implications of disturbingly high rates of domestic violence exposure among young children, Groves, Zuckerman, Marans, and Cohen (1993) noted that efforts to identify these "silent victims," who do not manifest conspicuous physical symptoms, should occur at the broad-based level of primary care. The authors noted that for preschool children who have limited capacity to verbalize their experiences, physicians should ask parents about their children's exposure to violence.

Domestic violence and abuse are characterized by direct, harmful, negative input that may worsen parent–child relationships, challenge the parent's ability to provide cognitive stimulation, and create an unsafe environment that prohibits child exploration. Such violence often co-occurs with the experience of neglect, which in contrast is defined by chronic inadequate input. The mechanisms by which neglect increases the risk of problems in cognitive development may be distinct from those of violence and abuse. For example, the long-term lack of stimulation that is a defining characteristic of neglect may restrict brain maturation, which in turn would lead to cognitive and linguistic deficits. Although research has yet to parse out the differential consequences of violence exposure and neglect, many studies have demonstrated that children who do not receive adequate stimulation in the first years of life experience atypical cognitive and language development (Pechtel & Pizzagalli, 2011). Ultimately, neglected children demonstrate poorer reading and math achievement in the school-age years (De Bellis, Hooper, Spratt, & Woolley, 2009).

THE IMPACT OF TRAUMA ON SOCIOEMOTIONAL DEVELOPMENT

It is now well established that the socioemotional harm of experiences such as maltreatment and domestic violence most often lasts longer and is more debilitating than the immediate physical harm (Aber & Cicchetti, 1984; Toth & Cicchetti, 2013). One example of this noted in early work is that the socioemotional harm of early trauma may extend across time and people, with violence exposure potentiating aggressive behavior toward others (Widom, 1989). From birth to 5 years, children move from complete dependency on caregivers to actively participating in social interactions, initiating play and conversations, and forming friendships. As emotional expressions become more complex and distinguishable, friends and family react to children in new ways; with the increasing ability to discriminate and label emotions, children are better able to respond to caregivers and friends. These changes are highly adaptive, promoting bonding and survival. For example, at around 8 to 12 months, children begin to distinguish the facial expressions of their caregivers to navigate frightening situations (Baldwin & Moses, 1996). As they grow older, they form friendships that broaden their social skills and provide emotional support.

Because development in the social and emotional domains is interdependent, disruptions due to trauma in either domain can create a cycle of worsening function. As in other areas of development, caregivers play a critical role in socioemotional development, serving to protect children from or potentially aggravate the experience of adversity. Children of maltreating caregivers or caregivers who are traumatized themselves are highly vulnerable to disruptions in socioemotional development and may manifest immediate and long-term problems in emotion regulation and relationships.

Trauma and Emotion Regulation

The study of emotion regulation, or individuals' implicit or effortful actions that up- or down-regulate an emotional response, has increased dramatically over the last decades (Gross, 2013). Although children who successfully regulate their emotions can respond appropriately and flexibly to challenges, children who are dysregulated may be excessively emotional, have constricted or inappropriate emotions, and demonstrate aggressive or disruptive behavior. In addition to the immediate effects on emotional expression and behavior in early life, emotion dysregulation may lead to long-term psychopathology. Indeed, emotion dysregulation is the defining characteristic of mood and anxiety disorders and is typically a component of disorders such as ADHD and autism (Gross, 2013). Therefore, an understanding of how the ability to regulate emotion develops in the first years of life, as well as how stress and trauma can compromise this ability, is critical for prevention as well as the treatment of psychopathology.

Emotion regulation in early life is largely driven by interactions with caregivers (Calkins & Hill, 2007). In a process termed *co-regulation*, the actions of caregivers serve to continuously modulate the emotional experience of young children. Successful co-regulation is characteristic of sensitive caregiving and secure attachment relationships. Much like cognitive scaffolding, co-regulation helps children learn to eventually regulate their emotions independently. However, this process may be impaired when caregivers are themselves exposed to trauma. The capacity for a caregiver to cope with trauma and to maintain a positive caregiver–child relationship is critical for the development of child emotion regulation (Pat-Horenczyk et al., 2015).

Studies have provided support for this theory, with findings indicating that infants and young children of mothers with PTSD are at greater risk of problems with emotion regulation and concomitant internalizing and externalizing symptoms. Bosquet Enlow and colleagues (2012) found that 6-month-old infants of mothers with PTSD demonstrated poorer emotion regulation in response to the Still Face Paradigm, a structured interaction designed to elicit infant distress and challenge co-regulation (Tronick, Als, Adamson, Wise, & Brazelton, 1978). Emotion dysregulation was evidenced by atypical emotional expression, including extreme distress continuing after the stressor had ceased. Pointing to the consequences of emotion dysregulation, infants of mothers with PTSD also demonstrated greater externalizing and internalizing symptoms at 6 months and greater dysregulation symptoms at 13 months. These findings are mirrored in research examining associations between the maternal capacity to self-regulate emotions and that of their young children. Pat-Horenczyk and colleagues (2015) found, in a sample of Israeli mothers and children age 2 to 6 years, that maternal emotion regulation predicted child emotion regulation problems as measured by the Child Behavior Checklist—Dysregulation Profile (Achenbach & Rescorla, 2001). In fact, maternal emotion regulation explained the association between maternal PTSD and child dysregulation, indicating that it may be the impact of trauma on maternal emotion regulation, rather than psychopathology itself, that creates child risk of dysregulation.

Children of parents with mental health problems are more likely to experience mental health problems themselves (Hancock, Mitrou, Shipley, Lawrence, & Zubrick, 2013). Disruptions in maternal emotion regulation may be a central mechanism for the intergenerational transmission of psychopathology (Pat-Horenczyk et al., 2015). Other studies have indicated that mothers and children display emotional and physiological synchrony such that children may mimic the maladaptive regulation patterns of their mothers (LeMoult et al., 2015; Waters, West, & Mendes, 2014). Even after considerable time has passed, the traumatic experiences of mothers remain to mark the lives of their children. In a recent 21-year longitudinal study, Roberts and colleagues (2015) found that the offspring of mothers who experienced abuse were more likely to experience depression, a disparity that persisted through age 31 years. When treating young children exposed to trauma, it is crucial to consider the trauma histories of their caregivers.

Of great concern is that caregivers who report being abused are more likely to abuse their children (Widom, 1989), although it is critical to emphasize that "this is by no means a certainty" (Pears & Capaldi, 2001, p. 1440). "Safe, stable, nurturing" family relationships appear to break this cycle of abuse (Jaffee et al., 2013, p. 1). Maltreating caregivers, whether abusive or neglectful, pose serious risks for child emotion regulation because they fail to assist children in learning to self-regulate. On the contrary, children of maltreating caregivers may learn atypical strategies for managing their emotions that have short-term benefits but long-term costs. For example, those exposed to inconsistent caregivers may learn to amplify their emotions to elicit attention, whereas those exposed to abusive caregiving may learn to restrict their emotions to avoid interaction (Mikulincer, Shaver, & Pereg, 2003).

There is evidence that maltreatment results in diverse patterns of problematic emotion regulation. For example, Maughan and Cicchetti (2002) found that approximately 80% of children age 4 to 6 who had experienced maltreatment had dysregulated patterns of emotion regulation. Although some were undercontrolled or ambivalent in their emotions, others were overcontrolled and unresponsive. In a study of children with different attachment histories, Kochanska (2001) found that by 14 months children varied in their emotional expressions. Children with an anxious–resistant attachment style were the most fearful and became less joyful through 33 months, whereas avoidant children became more fearful, and disorganized children became angrier. These increases in negative emotion and decreases in positive emotion among insecurely attached children may precede the development of behavior problems and psychopathology. Indeed, the dysregulated patterns identified by Maughan and Cicchetti were associated with greater behavior problems and explained the association between maltreatment and internalizing symptoms in young children. In an investigation of preschool children exposed to sexual abuse, problematic emotion regulation fully mediated the relation between abuse exposure and externalizing problems (Langevin, Hébert, & Cossette, 2015).

Trauma and Attachment Relationships

Trauma in early childhood can disrupt the bonds or *attachments* young children form with their primary caregivers, with implications for behavior and emotion regulation. According to attachment theory, these bonds are critical for development (Bowlby, 1988). Parent–child relationships involve behaviors that maintain attachments and serve to regulate child physiology, emotion, and behavior. Specifically, proximity seeking, such as when children cry out for their caregivers, serves to solicit parental responses that relieve child distress and provide felt security (Osofsky, 1995). Once children attain security, they can shift toward play and exploration. The success of proximity seeking, however, depends on the sensitivity and responsiveness of attachment figures (Ainsworth, 1989). When parents are neglectful or abusive, children form atypical expectations about how attachment figures usually behave and about the value of the self. As Ainsworth, Blehar, Waters, and Wall (1978) demonstrated, insecure attachment relationships are characterized by maternal insensitivity and child behaviors that cling to, resist, or avoid parents who are perceived as unavailable or frightening.

As described in this chapter, successful co-regulation of child emotion in the context of the attachment relationship is key for adaptive development, including the child's ability to self-regulate at later ages and his or her resilience to psychopathology. Types of insecure attachment styles include avoidant and resistant attachment, as well as the more recently identified disorganized style (Carlson, 1998; Hesse & Main, 1999). Although suboptimal, the *avoidant* and *resistant* attachment styles involve strategies for coping with stress that have short-term benefits (Dozier, Meade, & Bernard, 2014). In contrast, the *disorganized* style, more common among children who have been neglected or abused (Cyr, Euser, Bakermans-Kranenburg, & van IJzendoorn, 2010), signifies the absence of an organized strategy for dealing with stress (Carlson, 1998). This attachment style is associated with pervasive psychobiological dysregulation and pronounced risk of immediate and long-term psychological problems (Dozier et al., 2014). Contributing to the onset and maintenance of these problems, children with disorganized attachments may also have greater trouble navigating future trauma. Indeed, a history of disorganized attachment in infancy predicts severity of PTSD symptoms in the late teenage years (Bosquet Enlow, Egeland, et al., 2014).

In addition to ignoring or frightening maternal behaviors, maternal exposure to maltreatment (Lyons-Ruth & Block, 1996), maternal psychopathology (Hayes, Goodman, & Carlson, 2013), and maternal attachment representations (van IJzendoorn, 1995) have been linked to insecure and disorganized attachment styles in children. These findings highlight the role that parents' experiences and psychological problems play in the development of parent–child relationships (Dozier, Bick, & Bernard, 2011). Children with disorganized attachments may also act in ways that push parents away—behavior that suggests they do not need their parents or cannot be comforted (Dozier et al., 2014). Most worrying is that parents may reciprocate this behavior (Stovall & Dozier, 2000), creating a recursive cycle in which children do not receive the care they need to recover. This recursive cycle typifies the notion that individuals with disorganized attachment experience "fright without solution" (Hesse & Main, 1999, p. 484).

Problems in emotion regulation and attachment relationships have been linked to the development of psychopathology. Although beyond the scope of this volume, disorders such as PTSD occur among young children exposed to early trauma. Childhood maltreatment may be the underlying cause of many types of psychopathology, with estimates that maltreatment accounts for 45% of the population attributable risk of childhood onset psychiatric disorders (Green et al., 2010). Recent work has focused on improving understanding of how mental health disorders manifest in early life and increasing the developmental sensitivity of criteria for diagnosis. It is important to emphasize, however, that many children exposed to trauma demonstrate resilience rather than developing mental health disorders (Bonanno, Westphal, & Mancini, 2011). Early interventions that focus on improving the caregiver–child relationship may increase the likelihood of resilience even in cases of exposure to severe violence and neglect.

CONCLUSION

Although each section of this chapter has described the impact of trauma in early life on a particular domain of functioning, it is important to note that development is highly integrated across biological, cognitive, linguistic, and socioemotional systems. For example, acquisition of executive function skills appears to assist not only in academic achievement but also in children's ability to regulate their emotions and succeed socially (National Scientific Council on the Developing Child, 2011). At the same time, aberrant patterns of biological reactivity and regulation may interfere with cognitive engagement and underlie problems with emotion regulation, behavior, and psychopathology. As Kendall-Tackett (2002) noted, "Health depends on a complex web of behaviors, thoughts, emotions, and social connections. . . . Abuse can influence health at any, or all, of these junctures, and these pathways will vary for each individual patient" (p. 725).

Current directions in research on the impact of trauma on development include the integration of multiple biological, cognitive, and socioemotional assessments to understand how changes in one area may influence the adaptive development of another. In addition, to improve screening and treatment, there is growing interest in delineating the differential effects of trauma based on amount, proximity, type, severity, chronicity, and timing of exposure. A comprehensive review of this research is beyond the scope of this chapter. However, given ongoing wars, frequent terrorist acts, and the increasing incidence of disasters, developmental psychologists are also examining how mass, community-level traumas affect child development, with critical implications for global posterity (Masten, Narayan, Silverman, & Osofsky, 2015; Masten & Osofsky, 2010). Although recent research has made considerable advances in understanding the impact of trauma on young children, this age group remains understudied. Future generations of scientists must recognize that research on young children is vital for understanding the etiology of health problems as well as preventing them. An interrelated issue centers on dispelling the notion that young children are not affected, forget about trauma, or grow out of negative reactions. It is abundantly clear that experiences in early life have a lasting impact.

In this chapter, we have provided considerable evidence that early caregiving, whether positive or negative, is crucial for long-term adaptation. When caregivers are the source of trauma, children may have particularly negative outcomes. However, even in these cases, resilience is possible. We have cited multiple studies demonstrating that children can recover when the caregiver–child relationship improves and that positive caregiving in the face of adversity protects children. Such findings are further highlighted in Chapter 3, where we detail specific treatment approaches that target the parent–child relationship.

Development in early life is highly complex, making work in this area both exciting and challenging. Young children are "moving targets" for researchers and clinicians (Franks, 2011); they are undergoing changes even as we implement assessments and treatments geared toward their current development stage. Although the existing research on the impact of trauma on development is by no means final and definitive, it supports the use of trauma-informed treatments in young children, particularly those that improve the parent–child relationship. In the Appendix, we summarize key points from this chapter that may be helpful when assessing and treating young children exposed to trauma. In the following chapters, we describe three evidence-based treatments that can be applied in evaluating and providing services for young children affected by traumatic events, and we provide illustrative clinical examples.

2

Child–Parent Psychotherapy

As reviewed in Chapter 1, the timing and quality of caregiving matter for children's long-term outcomes. Identifying mental health problems in young children under age 5 and providing early therapeutic services can prevent more serious problems from developing (Egger & Emde, 2011; Osofsky & Lieberman, 2011; Tronick & Beeghly, 2011). One of the most widely used psychotherapeutic approaches for young children is *child–parent psychotherapy* (CPP) (Lieberman, Ghosh Ippen, & Van Horn, 2015; Lieberman & Van Horn, 2005, 2008), an evidence-based treatment designed to help infants, young children, and their caregivers after exposure to trauma (Lieberman, Ghosh Ippen, & Van Horn, 2006; Toth, Maughan, Manly, Spagnola, & Cicchetti, 2002). The attachment system helps organize the child's response to danger and safety. Because emotional and behavior problems often relate to attachment and relationship

http://dx.doi.org/10.1037/0000030-003
Treating Infants and Young Children Impacted by Trauma: Interventions That Promote Healthy Development, by J. D. Osofsky, P. T. Stepka, and L. S. King

issues, CPP is designed to work with the child and caregiver to support and strengthen the attachment, with a focus on restoring trust, a sense of safety, and appropriate affect regulation. For young children exposed to trauma, CPP works to normalize trauma-related responses and return the child to a normal developmental trajectory.

Attention to the cultural values of the family, including differences in parenting goals, discipline beliefs, and developmental expectations, is important, with an emphasis on recognizing and respecting strengths based on diversity (Ghosh Ippen & Lewis, 2011; Lieberman et al., 2015). Interventions are tailored to the specific family and their context, with culture being an important part of the context (Lewis & Ghosh Ippen, 2004; Lieberman, 1990). Recent training in CPP has focused on integrating issues of diversity into treatment, including different ways of working with culturally diverse families. Clinicians are encouraged to modify strategies for engagement and treatment, depending on the needs and background of the family, while maintaining the core components of the treatment. The basic theoretical principles and core goals of CPP are thought to apply across diverse groups. The treatment has been used extensively with a wide range of minority groups: Latino (Mexican, Central, and South American), African American, and Asian (Chinese). Clinical and research data, including four randomized trials conducted with predominantly ethnic minority samples, document the efficacy of this approach with culturally diverse groups.

The philosophy underlying CPP is that the attachment system organizes children's responses to their environment, including traumatic experiences, and that problems in infancy are best addressed in the context of the attachment relationship. CPP is based on the premise that the child's relationship with the mother, father, or primary attachment figure represents the most important "port of entry" or opportunity for intervention to help support child development, with a particular focus on social and emotional development. CPP works with the parent or caregiver and child to facilitate increased emotional and behavioral regulation, which is particularly important for children exposed to trauma.

EVIDENCE BASE FOR CHILD–PARENT PSYCHOTHERAPY

CPP is included as an evidence-based treatment in the Mental Health and Substance Abuse Services Administration National Registry of Evidence-Based Programs and Practices on the basis of five randomized controlled trial studies. The research consistently found improved outcomes in families who received the intervention compared with a control group of families who received either no intervention or an alternative intervention (see http://nrepp.samhsa.gov). The first study investigated the quality of attachment, testing the hypothesis that CPP would improve the relationship for anxiously attached toddler–mother dyads (Lieberman, Weston, & Pawl, 1991). Half the group of anxiously attached toddler–mother dyads received CPP for a year, beginning when the toddlers were 12 months. The other half represented a nonintervention control group. The findings indicated that the toddlers in the intervention group were higher in goal-directed activity and lower in avoidance, resistance, and anger than the control group. Mothers in the intervention group showed more empathy and also interacted more with their children.

The second study investigated quality of attachment, cognitive development, and family climate in toddlers of depressed mothers. In this study, the effect of treatment with CPP was compared with standard treatment in influencing the attachment security of toddlers of depressed mothers. The findings indicated that following the intervention, toddlers of depressed mothers showed significant improvement in attachment security (Toth, Rogosch, Manly, & Cicchetti, 2006). In 2002, Toth and colleagues carried out the third study, which involved a randomized controlled trial with 122 multiethnic maltreating and nonmaltreating low-income families, comparing CPP with psychoeducational home visitation and community standard treatment. They also included a low-income comparison group. Using the MacArthur Story Stem Battery (Bretherton et al., 1990), they found that children in the CPP group showed significant declines in maladaptive representations relative to the other two groups as well as greater decreases in negative self-representations. Mother–child relationship expectations showed significant positive changes or trends relative to the other two groups.

The fourth study, carried out by Lieberman, Van Horn, and Ghosh Ippen (2005), investigated posttraumatic stress disorder (PTSD), behavior problems, and maternal symptoms in preschooler–mother dyads exposed to domestic violence. The sample consisted of 75 multiethnic preschoolers with a mean age of 4 years. Dyads were assigned to weekly CPP for a year or community-based services plus case management. The findings indicated that the CPP group showed significant improvements in total behavior problems, traumatic stress symptoms, and diagnostic status. In addition, there were significant improvements in maternal avoidance and trends toward improvement in maternal PTSD symptoms after a year. A follow-up 6 months posttreatment showed that the improvement in symptoms persisted.

The fifth study, carried out by Cicchetti, Rogosch, and Toth (2006), investigated the quality of attachment and hypothalamic–pituitary–adrenal axis regulation in maltreated infants. The families studied consisted of 137 dyads randomly assigned to CPP, a psychoeducational parenting intervention, or community standard treatment. The fourth group of 52 nonmaltreated infants and their mothers comprised a low-income comparison. Children receiving CPP and those receiving a psychoeducational parenting intervention both showed increases in the security of attachment compared with the other two groups. When the groups were combined for further analysis, Cicchetti, Rogosch, Toth, and Sturge-Apple (2011) found that maltreated infants who received either CPP or a psychoeducational parenting intervention developed patterns of cortisol regulation resembling those of nonmaltreated infants, whereas infants in the community standard treatment group showed progressive dysregulation. In a follow-up study, Stronach, Toth, Rogosch, and Cicchetti (2013) found that children who received CPP continued to have higher rates of secure attachment and lower rates of disorganized attachment than those in the community standard treatment group.

THE COURSE OF CHILD–PARENT PSYCHOTHERAPY TREATMENT

When a young child and caregiver enter treatment, the most important first step, as in other psychotherapeutic work, is to develop a therapeutic relationship. A clinician must first assess the caregiver's appropriateness to participate in CPP. An important, but difficult, component of the evaluation and early treatment is to gain information about the traumatic events the child has experienced, as well as the caregiver's trauma history (Fraiberg, Adelson, & Shapiro, 1975; Lieberman, Padron, Van Horn, & Harris, 2005). Information about trauma is crucial to the early therapeutic process because gathering such information allows the clinician to bring the trauma into CPP and, over time, to place it in perspective. It provides a way to communicate to both the child and caregiver that it is acceptable to tell their story and that the clinician will listen. Over time, it helps to destigmatize the idea of talking about the traumatic experience. Early work of CPP involves helping the parent or caregiver understand the connection between the traumatic experience, emotions, and behavior displayed by the young child, helping them understand that behavior has meaning. As noted throughout this volume, if a young child experiences a traumatic event, it can influence not only their immediate emotions and behaviors but also disrupt adaptive development. A major goal of treatment is to work with the caregiver and child through the relationship to return to a normal developmental trajectory.

In CPP, there are child-focused, adult-focused, and relationship goals. For the child, the main goal is to support positive mental health, which is best done by working through the relationship. Restoring safety and emotional security are crucial, with these goals taking precedence over all others. Because trauma interferes with trust and can affect safety, a major goal of the therapeutic work is to repair emotionally damaging perceptions and interactions in the relationship. This goal is particularly important for children who have been abused or neglected or those with parents dealing with substance abuse or mental illness. The work of CPP will help the young child learn to manage negative emotions and express feelings in healthier ways. In the process of the work, the clinician also addresses the caregiver's psychological functioning and parenting skills and abilities. Important inclusion criteria for CPP include (a) addressing behavioral and emotional difficulties in children age 0 to 6 years; (b) helping a child or family that has experienced a traumatic event; and (c) having a caregiver who is able, willing, and appropriate in terms of mental health, cognitive capacity, and motivation to participate in treatment.

TREATMENT PLANNING FOR CHILD–PARENT PSYCHOTHERAPY

CPP is a joint enterprise between the family and the therapist, involving assessment, treatment, and reassessment during treatment. The goals are hierarchical, depending on the needs of the family. During the initial stages of treatment and at various times throughout the process, the assessment informs the goals. Treatment planning is always directed toward safety first, both physical and psychological. *Physical safety* may mean the child and parent are safe, with reasonable housing and food. In cases of domestic violence, having protective orders would be included, if needed, and for substance abuse, being compliant with treatment and case plans. *Psychological safety* also may include protecting the child and parent from other maladaptive exposures and influences, including substance abuse and mental illness.

The parent may need help learning ways to support her or his child or her- or himself in affect regulation, limit setting, and methods of providing appropriate discipline. Early goals of a trauma-focused treatment may include helping the caregiver recognize traumatic reactions or learn coping strategies to help with symptoms, trauma reminders, and triggers. Throughout treatment, the clinician provides guidance in the ways the caregiver can make meaning of the traumatic experiences for the child and respond in ways to enhance safety, emotional regulation, healthy attachment, and understanding. This work may take the form of a traditional "trauma narrative" and/or be a series of brief moments during which the caregiver connects themes from the child's symbolic play to emotional states and behaviors. Treatment goals must be prioritized according to the experience and needs of the parent or caregiver and child. During treatment planning it is important to keep in mind the goals of treatment: (a) encourage the child's return to a normal developmental trajectory that includes engagement in current activities and planning for future goals; (b) maintain regular levels of affect arousal; (c) achieve reciprocity in intimate relationships; (d) restore and strengthen the relationship between child and parent; (e) help restore attachment and appropriate affect; and (f) improve cognitive, behavioral, and emotional functioning.

FOUNDATIONS OF CHILD–PARENT PSYCHOTHERAPY

CPP was developed on the basis of multitheoretical perspectives integrating attachment, psychoanalytic, family systems, developmental, and trauma theories. This therapeutic approach is unique, using the dual lens of trauma and attachment and recognizing the primacy of attachment. The principal components include joint child–caregiver sessions centered on child's free play and spontaneous caregiver–child interactions. The therapist serves as a "conduit" or translator between the caregiver and child to create shared meanings. The interventions target child and/or parent behaviors and parent–child interactions that include ports of entry or opportunities for intervention. A focus of the sessions is to facilitate shared affect starting with simple strategies that may be as basic as supportive psychoeducation. As the therapy progresses, more complex interventions are included, such as interpretation to facilitate change. A primary role of the CPP provider is to act as a translator between parent and child to promote safety and trust, help the parent understand the meaning behind the child's behavior and play, and simultaneously help the child understand the significance behind the parent's behavior and emotional expressions.

WHAT IS NOT A CHILD–PARENT PSYCHOTHERAPY INTERVENTION

In comparing and contrasting CPP with other therapeutic interventions, it is important to recognize and acknowledge what is not considered an intervention appropriate to CPP. It is always important to remember that the therapist's role is not to be a better parent than the parent. The therapist has to be careful not to "take over" the parenting role for a parent by playing and interacting with the child in the place of the parent. The only exception to this situation is if the issue of safety emerges during the session. Another way a therapist can become a better parent than the parent is in modeling positive parenting to the parent through direct interaction with the child by essentially taking over when reflective commenting and questioning would be more appropriate. Because therapists who choose to work with young children tend to be "child oriented," there also may be a tendency to play with the child without involving the parent and just having him or her watch. This type of interaction is not compatible with a relationship-based CPP intervention. Another tendency can be engaging the parent in conversation—or more often, the parent wanting to "take over the session" to discuss her or his concerns about the child. Adult conversation during therapy without the age-appropriate inclusion of the child is an inappropriate component of CPP.

THE PHASES OF CHILD–PARENT PSYCHOTHERAPY

Assessment and Engagement

The assessment process begins like any other therapeutic process: with developing a therapeutic alliance with the client—in this case both a parent or caregiver and young child. It is recommended, if at all possible, that the first session include only the parent or caregiver to gather crucial background information and history without the discussion being inhibited by the presence of the child. To initiate treatment, it is important to learn about the reason the parent or caregiver is seeking treatment for the child and to gather information about the child's symptoms, demographic information, and developmental history. Following the initial session, the therapist observes and evaluates the child and the caregiver during free and structured play. These observations allow the clinician to learn more about how the child relates to and interacts with the parent or caregiver. It is also recommended that the therapist gather as much information as possible through interviews and observations about the child's behavior and reactions in other settings such as day care, preschool, and with other caregivers. By observing the child, the clinician can also learn about the child's developmental functioning, including age appropriate skills, regulatory capacity, the quality of the relationship, and areas of strength and weakness. During the observational part of the assessment, the clinician should be attuned to trauma-related symptoms such as repetitive play, talking about traumatic events, hypervigilance, arousal, avoidance, and other trauma-related symptoms.

During the assessment process, the clinician obtains information about the trauma history of the child from interviews with the parent or caregiver, observations, and also, if possible, using a structured interview such as the Traumatic Events Screening Inventory–Parent Report Revised (Ghosh Ippen et al., 2002). The therapist also learns about the trauma history of the parent and, if deemed important, obtains an assessment of parental depression. Learning about parental beliefs and practices is important, as are parent perceptions of the child, including the difficulties the parent is having with the child's behaviors or reactions. Caregivers who may be included in the assessment and treatment include grandparents, foster parents, adoptive parents, and other family members. If older siblings are involved, they may be included as well as relatives such as aunts and uncles, close friends if they are significant caregivers for the child, and any other individuals who play a significant role in the child's life. To assess which adults should be included in treatment, the clinician has to learn who the primary attachment figures are for the child and who provides daily care. For all caregivers, it is important to know who keeps the child safe and whether his or her emotional well-being is affected by this person's actions. The clinician has to assess the potential for the stability of the placement over time. As part of that assessment, it is important to determine whether the caregiver is competent to understand the child's experience, is emotionally or mentally stable enough to provide predictable responses to the child's emotions and needs, and is motivated to provide responsive and sensitive care.

Setting the Child–Parent Psychotherapy Trauma Frame

In initiating CPP, it is important to have a feedback session with the caregiver before the session introducing the child to CPP. During the feedback session, the trauma frame for the treatment is discussed with the parent, as well as, collaboratively, working on how it will be presented to the child. This is the session in which the clinician determines whether CPP will be appropriate, according to the parent's reaction to feedback.

The first session with the child and parent or caregiver following the assessment must include an explanation to the child, which the parent also hears, of the reason she or he is being brought to therapy. If the reason is directly related to trauma, the trauma should be specifically named and the concerns related to the trauma elaborated for the child and the parent or caregiver. As previously noted, to gain important information and frame the conversation so that the parent or caregiver is prepared to react and respond in a supportive manner for the child, the therapist and parent should meet alone and discuss the approach before the session. Also, during the session, the therapist should support the parent as much as possible to help him or her be able to take the lead. As the therapeutic process begins, if appropriate, the therapist chooses toys that may elicit themes related to why the parent and child are coming to treatment. Themes may be shown through play with any toys and are sometimes not apparent to the therapist or parent; however, having toys that promote reciprocal play such as a doll's house, aggressive and benign or kind animals, play food, or a family group of dolls may help elicit themes.

In the first dyadic session, while providing feedback and introducing the child to CPP, the potential themes that may emerge are discussed to assess both the child's and parent's reactions and the support provided to the child within the trauma frame. Encouraging play, reciprocity, and shared affect between parent and child is an important part of the process of CPP, and during the play, the therapist will observe and watch for *ports of entry* or opportunities for intervention. The interventions may be addressed to the child, the parent, or the relationship; however, it is crucial for the therapist to recognize that all interventions will be heard and processed by both the parent and the child. The goal of the intervention is to promote increased understanding within the relationship for the parent or caregiver of the child and the child of the caregiver.

Trauma Processing in Child–Parent Psychotherapy

A key part of the therapeutic work is to include direct, clear, and age-appropriate acknowledgment of trauma and the possible emotional and behavioral responses that can follow, including trauma triggers, avoidance, and emotional and behavioral dysregulation. A goal of the joint play is to help the child and parent learn to understand and verbalize feelings related to the traumatic experiences or, for younger preverbal children, show their feelings through play. The interventions are designed to meet the needs of the parent, child, and parent–child relationship as much as possible, addressing ongoing understanding and communication of all the participants. Through the therapeutic work, the parent can learn to validate the child's emotional experience and help him or her in regulating emotions and behaviors. This activity begins the process of creating a joint narrative about the traumatic experiences to reestablish trust and safety.

Most often the work of CPP is done with the child, caregiver, and therapist in the room together, and this is the preferred mode for the therapeutic work. However, at times, the therapist may find it useful to have other structured sessions as well, including caregiver–child sessions with collateral parent sessions, separate sessions with either the parent or child, and even individual sessions with the child if the caregiver is unavailable for a period. However, it is crucial for the therapist to understand that although CPP is a dyadic treatment, including both child and parent, if a choice has to be made about how to maintain a therapeutic alliance, the relationship with the parent or caregiver must be considered first, mainly because maintaining a relationship with the adult is essential for the child to come to treatment. The relationship with the parent or caregiver begins during the assessment process, with the therapist conveying an understanding that the caregiver is an important part of the treatment process.

The Trauma Narrative

Before beginning to work with a caregiver and child to create a trauma narrative, it is crucial to understand and embrace the idea that young children have to be understood in the context of their relationships. If the relationship has been abusive, neglectful, or traumatizing in other ways, it is important to take all of these components into account. The clinician working together with the parent has to be able to "hold" the dysregulated emotions and behaviors, understand that they have "meaning," and help both parent and child learn to modulate and then express the feelings through play and language. The traumatic experience may manifest itself through symbolic play and behavior, behavioral reenactment, somatic reexperiencing, or verbalization. Optimally, the development of the trauma narrative will be a mix of planned, didactic, and structured development using words as well as spontaneous, unplanned behavioral reactions.

The parent or caregiver is prepared, as is the clinician; the clinician is flexible and open and will play a role in expanding and deepening the narrative experience. A major component of preparation for the clinician is the assessment process described in detail earlier. Sometimes the child may be more ready than the parent to describe the traumatic event either using words or play. A key role the clinician plays is to increase the parent's capacity to witness the play and words of the child and join in with the child. Again, as in all CPP work, the clinician must work together with both the parent and child, supporting the needs of both members of the dyad. To help support the child and parent in creating a trauma narrative, it is important that the parent and clinician are able to tolerate ambiguity and create meaning, even if it is imperfect, recognizing that the development of the narrative is not an end in itself.

CORE INTERVENTIONS OF CHILD–PARENT PSYCHOTHERAPY

Ports of Entry and Domains of Intervention

Ports of entry are the *when* of CPP intervention, and the domains of intervention are the *where* and *how*. Central to CPP is a focus on both ports of entry (opportunities for intervention) and domains of intervention. It is crucial when working with trauma that the child and parent with whom you are working are in a safe environment and situation to carry out the therapeutic work, which is the first principle of CPP. Therefore, at times, a therapist must focus on safety issues before other concerns. For example, if the mother has been and is still in a relationship that is not safe (i.e., involving domestic violence), the therapist has to deal with these concerns with the mother before focusing on treatment with the dyad. Safety and issues of trust must be addressed for the child and parent individually and as a dyad.

Ports of entry are opportunities for intervention: when and where the clinician intervenes. In deciding how to intervene, it is important to begin with the simplest intervention the clinician believes will make a difference for both the child and parent. Although the theoretical background of CPP is important for the work, the ports of entry are not based on a particular theory. CPP does not have a session-by-session predetermined agenda; rather, the course of treatment is determined by the needs of the child and parent at that specific time in treatment. For example, well-timed developmental guidance may be the most effective intervention. A therapeutic intervention that can be incorporated into CPP early in the treatment is *speaking for baby*, in which the therapist puts into words for the parent or caregiver what the young child may be communicating through his or her behavior. For example, the therapist may speak for the young child, saying, "I love it when you play with me" or "It's fun when we sing a song together" or "I may look like I can do that myself, but I'm little, and I need your help." Speaking for baby provides an important way for the parent to gain increased understanding of her or his baby's needs and help the parent learn that behavior, even disruptive behavior, has meaning for the baby (Carter, Osofsky, & Hann, 1991). It is also an intervention that is relatively easy for the therapist to learn early in the course of dyadic work and is effective because the therapist is not put in a position of having to either tell a parent what to do or do it for her. *Reflective guidance*—reflecting what the child or parent may be feeling—is also a useful intervention to incorporate in the treatment.

It is important to keep in mind when doing CPP that if simple interventions do not seem to make a difference for the child and parent, as in other therapeutic work, the clinician should choose the interventions that address resistance, mistrust, or psychological obstacles. In work with CPP, it is essential that the therapist use careful observation with young children, who often do not have the language to express their needs. Building rapport and timing the interventions appropriately are extremely important. Working to understand the child's and parents' representational (internal) worlds and using interpretation usually come later in the treatment but are important components of the work. In selecting a port of entry, the therapist has to consider his or her relationship with the family, the phase of treatment, the timing within the session, and the affect being displayed by the child and parent.

One of the most important domains of intervention is play, and the therapist's role is to help the parent understand that play has meaning and is a way young children show how they feel and how they experience their world. The therapist's role is to support the parent in playing with her child, learning how to follow the child's lead, and ultimately understanding that children learn through play. It is important for the therapist also to support the parent's emotional response during play, especially if it is trauma focused, which may be difficult for the parent to observe and understand. Having completed a trauma screen with the child helps the therapist better understand the meaning of the child's play, whereas knowing the parent's trauma history sensitizes the therapist to types of play content that may be difficult for the caregiver to integrate and respond to sensitively. Later in the therapeutic process, the parent plays a key role in understanding and helping the child create a trauma narrative through different play modalities.

The second domain of intervention is helping in the regulation of biological rhythms and sensory integration. A child may be dysregulated at times because a parent is also dysregulated or, more commonly, because a parent does not know what may be most helpful in supporting the child's behavioral and emotional regulation. Some parents need help in establishing routines for their child, such as mealtimes, naps, bedtime, and child care or preschool. It is important for the therapist to engage the parent in this process to learn what may be interfering with her or his ability to maintain a schedule. At times, the parent may need the therapist's help in controlling and regulating the child's behaviors or emotions, but if this type of intervention is needed, it must be discussed and worked through with the parent. Parents may benefit from intervention regarding their responses to the young child's fearfulness, or, even more common, aggression. For fearful behavior that may be a result of exposure to trauma, the therapist has to support the parent in learning and providing helpful and appropriate responses. The clinician should also help the parent, who may be more likely to dismiss the child's fearfulness, to understand possible reasons for the behaviors and emotional reactions.

Childhood Aggression and CPP

Displaying some aggressive behaviors is a normal part of development for young children. Toddlers may hit, kick, or bite when they have strong feelings but do not yet have the language to express themselves more effectively or the self-control to keep themselves from acting on the feelings. Parents and other adults help young children control their behaviors by staying calm, being consistent and clear about unacceptable behavior, and talking with their children. When young children are exposed to trauma, a common reaction is aggression, because they may have witnessed the aggressive behavior of an adult and are copying the behavior and also because they have strong feelings as a result of the trauma that they cannot express in words. Therefore, the usual ways to deal with the aggressive behaviors often are not effective with young traumatized children. Furthermore, the parents or caregivers may also be traumatized themselves. For those reasons, aggression is a common problem influencing a parent or caregiver to seek treatment. Often the parent needs assistance in learning ways to deescalate and ultimately stop the aggressive behavior. The therapist can help the parent learn to redirect the aggressive behavior and also understand ways to help their child express anger in nonhurtful ways. Through these therapeutic interventions, the parent may come to understand that the child's behavior has meaning and that being aggressive may be one of the few ways the child has to communicate feelings. It is helpful if the therapist can create an atmosphere in which the aggressive behaviors can be discussed and alternative behaviors considered and practiced. Sometimes the aggressive behavior may be a response to angry or hurtful behavior on the part of the parent. In this circumstance, discussing the behavior and the situation it creates can be done while still being sensitive to the parent's feelings.

Other domains of intervention may relate to the parent's aggression or parental absence. Here, it is important for the therapist to work with both the child and parent to understand that frightening and upsetting things may happen and that they can be talked about, rather than the therapist relying only on education or the parent using direct intervention. For children who are seeking treatment due to trauma or loss, both transitions during the session and at the time the session ends may be difficult for them. This offers an opportunity to help both parent and child learn to talk about the upsetting traumas or losses that have occurred. It also allows both of them to think more about planning and preparation for expected transitions and losses such as those that occur during and at the end of every session and, importantly, is an area for building trust and an opportunity for sensitive work during CPP.

Termination of treatment is another domain of intervention, and it is important to recognize that, at least in some instances, it may be the first experience the child—or parent—has had of a nontraumatic separation or loss. Therefore, preparation and planning with both the child and parent are crucial for the process of terminating treatment.

How to Maintain Fidelity to the Child–Parent Psychotherapy Model

The developers of CPP (Lieberman et al., 2015) recognized that fidelity to CPP must be multidimensional, involving fidelity to content, but they also recognized that individual emotional, intrapsychic, and interpersonal processes play key roles in implementation. The CPP clinician must notice feelings in the moment, find emotional links between experiences, uphold the legitimacy of the parent's and child's different motives and needs, become a translator when explaining the parent's and child's conflicting agendas to each other, name the trauma, dare to speak about what hurts, remember the suffering under the rage, take care of him- or herself, offer kindness, and encourage hope (Lieberman et al., 2015, p. 191). On the basis of the complexity of the therapeutic stance required by a well-trained CPP provider, fidelity is conceptualized as involving six interconnected strands. These six strands of fidelity are useful during CPP training. They serve as underpinnings to the process of CPP, helping to guide the work of the clinician just as the supervisor provides guidance and support to the therapist. Together, the clinician and supervisor consider ways to support the family. The fidelity strands are as follows:

- *Reflective practice fidelity.* The clinician must deal with the inevitable emergence of strong emotional reactions that can be stimulated by interactions between the parent and child as well as in the dyad with the therapist. It is important that the clinician is aware of these feelings so that they do not interfere with the treatment during which the clinician has to remain neutral and emotionally available to the child and parent.

- *Emotional process fidelity.* The clinician has to help the parent and child explore their complex feelings toward the adversity they have experienced and learn what their responses may mean to achieve a healthier adaptation. Trauma-related content can provoke strong reactions in both the child and the parent. The therapist must be able to both assist the caregiver in naming and helping regulate their child's emotional reactions and support the caregiver in reflecting on her emotional status and coping responses.

- *Dyadic relational fidelity.* The clinician has to support the relationship between the parent and child to help the latter recover from trauma and get back on track developmentally. Clinicians must consider the impact of their words, actions, and inactions on both the child and the caregiver. Specifically, attention has to be paid to how the interventions will be experienced by the caregiver and the child and how they may enhance or weaken the attachment relationship.

- *Trauma framework fidelity.* In CPP, the clinician works to identify and address the child's and parent's experiences of trauma to help them both heal and support the child's normal developmental trajectory. The clinician seeks to enhance the caregiver's effectiveness by helping him or her understand the behaviors and reactions of the dyad in the context of their histories. They may need support in making meaning of terrifying experiences for the child and also may need help in differentiating past situations from present circumstances.

- *Procedural fidelity.* The clinician implements the key procedures that help guide and organize the therapeutic work, including both screening (paper and pencil) and observational measures. The assessment will include not only developmental components but also, and importantly, evaluation of traumatic experiences for both the child and the caregiver.

- *Content fidelity.* The clinician follows the overall goals of treatment but is also flexible in tailoring the treatment to meet the needs of the child and the caregiver.

THE IMPORTANCE OF REFLECTIVE SUPERVISION IN CHILD–PARENT PSYCHOTHERAPY

Reflective supervision is a key component of training and effective work in CPP (Osofsky & Weatherston, 2016). Unlike more directive supervision, being reflective means stepping back from the immediate, intense experience of therapeutic work with traumatized infants, young children, and their families to take the time to wonder what the experience means. What kinds of feelings does this work evoke in ourselves, and what does it tell us about the young child or family we are seeing? Reflective supervision in the course of training with a trusted supervisor helps the clinician examine thoughts and feelings that emerge in working with a family and identify interventions that best meet the family's goals for self-sufficiency, growth, and development. To carry out reflective supervision most effectively, it is important for the supervisor and supervisee to create an environment that is trusting and safe, marked by regularity and consistency. It involves collaboration—that is, a sharing of power and responsibility and open communication between the supervisor and supervisee. In such an environment, it is safe to explore a range of emotions, thoughts, and feelings from positive to negative and to learn how personal reactions to the situation may play an important role and help in understanding the meaning of the therapeutic work.

CONCLUSION

CPP is an evidence-based intervention designed for working with infants, young children, and their caregivers when a traumatic event has been experienced. The young child may be having problems with attachment, behavior or emotional regulation, and/or mental health problems. CPP is designed to support and strengthen the relationship and through that process help the child to resume a normal developmental trajectory. The relationship-based approach provides the space for the infant or child and parent to work through developmental and relationship struggles through play. Also central to the process is engaging the parent to be reflective about the child's inner world of feelings, thoughts, and desires through which the caregiver gains an increased understanding of the effects of trauma on the young child and her or his emotional responses. Reflective supervision for the therapist also plays a key role in training and therapeutic work in CPP by helping her or him support the caregiver.

3

Attachment and Biobehavioral Catch-Up Intervention

The *attachment and biobehavioral catch-up (ABC) intervention,* developed by Mary Dozier and colleagues at the University of Delaware, has a strong evidence base for treatment of young children exposed to trauma. The ABC intervention has been shown to be effective in improving a variety of outcomes among maltreated children (Dozier, Meade, & Bernard, 2014). Importantly, positive effects of ABC have been observed across different samples and settings, including maltreated children living with foster parents and those living with birth parents. Dissemination of ABC is also expanding, with careful efforts to maintain protocol adherence and treatment fidelity (Caron, Bernard, & Dozier, 2016). Recently, the intervention was successfully implemented by community agencies (Caron, Weston-Lee, Haggerty, & Dozier, 2015; Roben, Dozier, Caron, & Bernard, in press). In this chapter, we present an up-to-date review of ABC, integrating knowledge and findings from a number of scientists and

http://dx.doi.org/10.1037/0000030-004
Treating Infants and Young Children Impacted by Trauma: Interventions That Promote Healthy Development, by J. D. Osofsky, P. T. Stepka, and L. S. King

clinicians who have designed, implemented, and evaluated this evidence-based intervention.

ABC is similar to child–parent psychotherapy (CPP) in that its theoretical base is attachment theory. Specifically, ABC focuses on decreasing the disorganized attachment style described in Chapter 1. *Disorganized attachment* is common among young children exposed to maltreatment and is identified by the lack of a coherent strategy for regulation (Bakermans-Kranenburg, van IJzendoorn, & Juffer, 2005), such that children with disorganized attachment styles present with pervasive dysregulation. ABC differs from CPP in that it is specifically designed for maltreated young children aged 6 to 24 months, with a focus on decreasing problems with attachment and psychobiological regulation that characterize this group (Dozier, Bick, & Bernard, 2011). By intervening with infants and toddlers—a group that is disproportionately vulnerable to maltreatment—ABC has the potential to foster recovery and prevent more serious problems from developing.

The relatively brief duration of the ABC intervention, comprising 10 one-hour sessions, as well as the nonthreatening focus on improving the parent–child relationship, facilitates parent engagement (Dozier et al., 2014). The 10 ABC sessions are conducted in the home with both parent and child present, which Dozier and colleagues (2014) noted as essential to the efficacy of the intervention. The theory is that when parents learn skills in their natural environments they are more likely to both use and generalize them. ABC is guided by empirical findings about the needs of young children who have been maltreated and the processes that can improve their outcomes (Dozier et al., 2014).

TARGETS OF THE ABC INTERVENTION

Although maltreatment in early life and the development of disorganized attachment pose serious risks for adaptive development, improving the parent–child relationship may help trauma-exposed children to change in positive ways. Children's attachment styles are not fixed; even after they have been maltreated, they can go on to develop secure attachments associated with effective regulatory strategies (Dozier, Stoval, Albus, &

Bates, 2001). ABC focuses on improving the parent–child relationship by increasing positive behaviors and decreasing negative behaviors among parents at risk of maltreating their children (Bernard, Dozier, Bick, Lewis-Morrarty, Lindhiem, & Carlson, 2012; Dozier et al., 2014).

Target 1: Cultivating Nurturance

The first target of ABC is to help parents cultivate nurturance so that they can become more sensitive to children's distress. *Nurturance* was defined by Bernard, Meade, and Dozier (2013) as the quality of parental responses to child distress, including the parents' ability to help children feel safe. Although many studies do not differentiate between parental sensitivity when children are distressed versus when children are calm or at play, sensitivity to child distress (i.e., nurturance) may be particularly important for the development of secure attachments (Bernard et al., 2013). Dozier and colleagues (2014) emphasized that children who have not been maltreated can form organized attachments to nonnurturing caregivers. Maltreated children, however, need nurturance to recover from their negative experiences.

Target 2: Cultivating Synchrony

The second target of ABC is to help parents be more sensitive during non-distress situations (e.g., play) by cultivating synchrony. Bernard and colleagues (2013) defined *synchrony* as the extent to which a parent "follows the child's lead" (p. 6) and supports child autonomy by responding contingently to the child's bids. They emphasized that the "serve and return" metaphor (National Scientific Council on the Developing Child, 2012) is helpful for illustrating synchronous interactions (Bernard et al., 2013). A child action such as moving toward a new toy can be understood as a *serve*, which evokes a timely parental response such as naming the toy, understood as a *return*. Although cognitive deficits may be a more obvious consequence of parental behavior that does not support exploration and autonomy, lower parental sensitivity during play has also been linked to socioemotional and physiological measures, such as greater affective distress and neurobiological dysregulation (Bosquet Enlow, King, et al., 2014). Indeed, Bernard and colleagues (2013) suggested that although nurturance may be a stronger predictor of attachment security, synchrony may be more important for behavioral and physiological regulation. ABC encourages parents to not just "respond" but rather to show "delight" and "genuine, unconditional positive affect and regard" to the child's bids (Dozier et al., 2014, p. 47).

Target 3: Reducing Frightening and Intrusive Behavior

The third target of ABC is to reduce the frightening and intrusive behaviors that maltreating parents are more likely to demonstrate. Frightening parenting behavior may lead to disorganized attachment because children's strategies for coping with stress break down when they both need their parents and are afraid of them (Carlson, 1998). ABC helps parents learn to recognize and reduce their frightening and intrusive behavior to both decrease disorganized attachment and enhance child regulation. Frightening behavior by parents may often be unintentional. For example, parents who have insecure attachment representations may demonstrate sudden and unexpected fear when reminded of their negative experiences with caregivers (van IJzendoorn, Schuengel, & Bakermans-Kranenburg, 1999). It is important for parents to learn that intrusive behavior, such as rapid and high arousal actions, can frighten young children even when the intent is positive. By teaching parents nurturance and synchrony, ABC helps parents learn alternative strategies for frightening and intrusive behavior (Dozier et al., 2014).

Psychobiological Regulation

In promoting synchrony and nurturance and in decreasing frightening behaviors, ABC has the ancillary goal of improving psychobiological regulation among maltreated children (Bernard, Dozier, et al., 2015). More nurturing and synchronous parents are better able to provide an environment that enhances child regulation, including regulation of the hypothalamic–pituitary–adrenal (HPA) axis. As described in Chapter 1, improving HPA-axis regulation may help children respond to and recover from stress flexibly and efficiently, decreasing their vulnerability to the negative consequences of environmental events and risk of psychopathology. Furthermore, the functioning of the HPA axis is associated with brain development. By improving psychobiological regulation, the ABC intervention may prevent negative physical and mental health outcomes among maltreated children.

DESIGN OF THE ABC INTERVENTION

The ABC intervention consists of 10 manualized sessions addressing the three targets of nurturance, synchrony, and frightening and intrusive behavior. Specific sessions also address the underlying thoughts and feelings of parents that may increase risk of maltreatment and insensitivity, as well as how to navigate child behaviors that push parents away (Dozier et al., 2011).

The goals of the ABC intervention are accomplished through manual-guided discussion, structured practice activities, video feedback, and "in-the-moment" comments by parent coaches (Dozier et al., 2014). Manual-guided discussions provide evidence-based explanations of the intervention targets and their importance (Roben et al., in press). In-the-moment comments, considered to be the most important feature of the intervention, occur about once per minute as parents engage in interactions with their children. Dozier and colleagues (2014) stated, "Manual content often takes a back seat to 'in the moment' comments" (p. 48), which are tailored to the evolving strengths of different families.

In-the-moment coaching provides parents with continuous feedback on the intervention targets. The three components of this feedback are (a) describing parenting behaviors clearly and specifically, (b) linking parenting behaviors with the intervention targets, and (c) highlighting how parenting behaviors affect children (i.e., why behaviors are important; Roben et al., in press; Meade, Dozier, & Bernard, 2014). Contrary to what parents may expect when enrolling in the intervention, in-the-moment comments are largely positive (Meade et al., 2014). This is especially true during initial sessions, when parents may exhibit limited nurturance and synchrony. With the goal of supporting positive interactions, parent coaches harness transitory positive actions within the context of overall negative behavior (Bernard et al., 2013; Meade et al., 2014). Dozier and colleagues (2014) provided the following illustration of an appropriate in-the-moment comment when a parent briefly displayed synchronous behavior: "He handed you that toy and you took it right from him. . . . That's a great example of you following his lead. . . . That lets him know he has an effect on the world" (p. 48). Bernard and colleagues (2013) provided another illustration of how a coach may respond to nurturing parental behavior: "He started to cry and you reached out to pick him up. . . . That's a great example of providing him with nurturance. . . . That is letting him know that he can trust you when he's upset" (p. 8). As sessions progress, parents become more skilled and rapport improves, and parent coaches begin to make comments that support, scaffold, and challenge parental behavior (Meade et al., 2014). Coaches may encourage following the lead, provide examples, and point out when parents are not being nurturing. For example, as Bernard and colleagues described, a coach may respond to a parent ignoring child distress by saying: "He looks pretty upset. This seems like one of those times when he may need your reassurance" (p. 8).

FIDELITY TO THE ABC INTERVENTION MODEL

For parent coaches, in-the-moment comments can be challenging because they require simultaneous focus on manualized content and observation of parent–child interactions (Meade et al., 2014). To help ensure fidelity to the model, all 10 sessions of the ABC intervention are video recorded so that not only parents but also coaches can receive video feedback about their performance. As described by Meade and colleagues (2014), parent coaches receive supervision as normal using the videos; in addition, they use the videos to qualitatively code 5-minute clips from their sessions. During coding, the coaches identify target parental behaviors as well as their responses to these behaviors. They note whether they missed opportunities to comment, whether their comments were "on target" (i.e., correctly matching parental behavior), and whether their comments were specific or too vague. This process ensures fidelity to the treatment model. With a single-subject design of a coach who provided 176 sessions to 19 families, Meade et al. found that training with video coding increased the frequency and usefulness of in-the-moment comments. In a community sample, Caron and colleagues (2016) found that greater frequency and quality of in-the-moment comments predicted larger gains in parental sensitivity and greater reductions in intrusiveness. In addition, when coaches made more comments, families were less likely to drop out of the intervention.

ASSESSMENT FOR THE ABC INTERVENTION

Qualitative coding of parenting behaviors during sessions is central to client assessment throughout the ABC intervention (Bernard et al., 2013). As noted earlier, coding involves coding of video clips of sessions. In addition, coaches code parent behaviors on standardized 5-point scales after each session, providing an additional continuous assessment of the dyad's strengths and needs (Dozier et al., 2014). Although some parents may struggle more with providing synchrony, others will encounter greater challenges to behaving in nurturing ways. Still others may be nurturing and synchronous when they respond but respond too infrequently, or they may not understand the difference between nurturance and synchrony. Given the flexibility of the ABC intervention to the dyad's evolving needs, patterns of parent behaviors that are captured during coding can be used to tailor subsequent sessions (Bernard et al., 2013). In addition, to assess overall improvement in synchrony, assessment for ABC includes a standardized play assessment before and after the 10-week intervention.

THE ABC INTERVENTION: SESSION-BY-SESSION

In Table 3.1, we provide an overview of the sessions of the ABC intervention, with more detailed descriptions of the 10 sessions as follows.

Table 3.1		
Overview of the Attachment and Biobehavioral Catch-Up Intervention by Session		
Session	Target(s)	Topics
1	Nurturance	Building understanding of the importance of nurturance when children are distressed
2		Providing nurturance even when children appear unsoothable or push parents away
3	Synchrony	Building understanding of the importance of synchrony during play
4		Allowing children to "take charge" during activities to promote their sense of control
5	Intrusiveness	Reading child cues for engagement and disengagement to reduce intrusiveness
6	Frightening behavior	Understanding the impact of frightening behavior and identifying alternative ways of responding
7	Nurturance, synchrony, intrusiveness, frightening behavior	Understanding how underlying thoughts and feelings affect responses to children
8		Overriding automatic reactions to children and choosing synchrony and nurturance
9		Consolidating gains and reinforcing the importance of touch during interactions
10		Consolidating gains and reinforcing the importance of reading children's emotions

Note. Data related to session content from Dozier, Bick, and Bernard (2011) and Dozier, Meade, and Bernard (2014).

Session 1: Nurturance

In Session 1, coaches introduce the goals of the intervention and describe the concept of nurturance. They emphasize the importance of nurturance for child well-being, including how nurturance helps children form a sense of control and safety. The coaches acknowledge that children's previous experiences with maltreatment may make them difficult to soothe, which can make parents feel ineffective. Coaches help parents understand the meaning of nurturance by asking them to reflect on recent interactions when their children were distressed, how they tended to respond, and what feelings and earlier experiences interfered with their ability to show nurturance.

Session 2: Nurturance When Child Behaviors Are Challenging

Building on Session 1, during Session 2, coaches focus more on how to provide nurturance even when children's behaviors are challenging. Coaches encourage parents to consider what challenging behaviors may mean in order to recognize children's underlying need for nurturance. They help parents to recognize their feelings when their children behave in secure versus insecure ways. Parents learn ways to respond with nurturance even when their children's behavior elicits negative or dismissive feelings.

Session 3: Synchrony

In Session 3, parent coaches introduce the concept of synchrony. Coaches describe the benefits for children of parents' following the lead, including how this promotes children's sense of having an "effect on the world" (Dozier et al., 2014, p. 48). When parents allow children to explore but also respond contingently and with delight, children perceive that the world is controllable and their actions can have positive effects. Video feedback is used to review the parent–child interactions, comment on opportunities for parents to display synchrony and delight, and point out whether parent responses were characterized by following or leading.

Session 4: Synchrony When Tasks Are Challenging

In Session 4, parents learn about how following the lead with delight increases children's sense of self-worth. Specifically, coaches discuss the importance of promoting children's autonomy by allowing them to "take charge" during appropriate but challenging activities (Dozier et al., 2014, p. 50). Coaches encourage parents to allow children to do aspects of challenging tasks independently. They review videos of shared activities to reinforce learning.

Session 5: Reducing Intrusiveness

In Session 5, parents learn about how intrusive behavior can frighten or overwhelm their children. Intrusive parents may ignore or be unaware of cues indicating that children want to slow down or disengage (Bakermans-Kranenburg et al., 2005). Therefore, coaches emphasize the importance of attending to child signals of being ready to interact or of being frightened. Coaches and parents review the video of interactions, with coaches commenting on child cues and praising parents for times they showed awareness of cues.

Session 6: Reducing Frightening Behavior

In Session 6, parents learn about how their behavior may frighten their children (Dozier et al., 2014). Coaches and parents discuss the importance of buffering children from scary situations—of serving as a source of safety rather than fear. An effective way to intervene is to help parents reflect on times when they were frightened during their childhood and then think about times when they may have frightened their children. Parents watch videos from past sessions, learn through observation, and discuss alternative strategies for responding.

Session 7: "Voices From the Past"

Session 7 is particularly sensitive because parents are first asked to think about how their underlying thoughts and feelings contribute to their children's behavioral problems. Dozier and colleagues (2011) noted the importance of using concrete terms when discussing how parents' thoughts and feelings affect their children. Coaches refer to parents' current representations of past attachment experiences as "voices from the past" (Dozier et al., 2011, p. 86). Coaches and parents review video clips from past sessions illustrating times when their thoughts and feelings may have challenged their ability to respond to their children with nurturance and synchrony.

Session 8: "Overriding" Automatic Reactions

In Session 8, coaches work with parents to help them use awareness of voices from the past to make their behaviors less automatic (Dozier et al.,

2014). Specifically, coaches help parents build the capacity to "override" their negative reactions to their children (Dozier et al., 2014, p. 51). Parents learn about how to consciously choose nurturance and synchrony even when their thoughts and feelings direct them to do otherwise. As parents take on this difficult task, they build on the knowledge gained in earlier sessions about the benefits of nurturance and synchrony for child well-being.

Session 9: "The Importance of Touch"

Session 9 reinforces understanding of the "importance of touch" in parent–child interactions (Dozier et al., 2011, p. 87). Parents at risk of maltreating their children may have adverse reactions to touch because of their experiences of abuse. At the same time, appropriate touch is especially important for children who have been maltreated because it promotes a sense of safety. As noted in Chapter 1, positive maternal presence helps buffer children from stress and negative emotions by improving neurobiological regulation (Gee et al., 2014). Other findings point to the specific benefits of maternal touch for infant physiology during both stress and play (Feldman, Singer, & Zagoory, 2010).

Session 10: Reading Emotions and Consolidating Gains

In the final ABC session, parents strengthen their knowledge about the importance of reading their children's emotional expressions and helping their children to feel comfortable expressing emotions (Dozier et al., 2011). This is a supportive session, designed to help parents consolidate gains related to awareness of their children's needs and how to provide nurturance and synchrony. Coaches emphasize that children should have the freedom to express both positive and negative emotions and that parents serve a critical role in helping children organize their emotions. Parents and coaches review videos depicting the progress parents have made in providing nurturance and synchrony and in decreasing frightening and intrusive behavior even when children express negative emotions.

EVIDENCE BASE FOR THE ABC INTERVENTION

Evidence from randomized controlled trials (RCTs) of the ABC intervention has indicated that it is effective in improving a variety of outcomes among maltreated children. These RCTs randomly assigned children with histories of maltreatment to the ABC intervention or to a control intervention providing parental education about children's motor, cognitive, and language development. Before the start of these interventions, parent and child functioning is assessed across a range of domains.

Results from RCTs conducted among foster children and Child Protective Services (CPS)–referred children living with their birth parents demonstrate that the ABC intervention is successful in accomplishing the primary goal of improving the parent–child relationship. At a 1-month follow-up, foster children who received the ABC intervention showed less avoidance of parents during a laboratory-based interaction designed to elicit attachment behaviors (Dozier et al., 2009), whereas foster mothers showed greater improvements in sensitivity at follow-up (Bick & Dozier, 2013). Similarly, CPS-referred children randomized to the ABC intervention showed lower rates of disorganized attachment and greater rates of secure attachment than those who received the control intervention (Bernard et al., 2012). Providing evidence that changes in parents' awareness and reactions to child cues may drive positive outcomes, Bernard, Simons, and Dozier (2015) found that CPS-referred mothers who received the ABC intervention showed greater event-related potential responses (an electroencephalogram measure) to children's emotional expressions (crying, laughing) than neutral expressions several years postintervention, whereas mothers in the control intervention did not. Moreover, this difference in brain activity was associated with greater maternal sensitivity.

There is also evidence from RCTs that children who receive the ABC intervention have improved socioemotional and cognitive outcomes. Specifically, these findings suggest that they are better at coping with stress (Lind, Bernard, Ross, & Dozier, 2014) and have greater executive function (Lewis-Morrarty, Dozier, Bernard, Terracciano, & Moore, 2012). Lind and colleagues (2014) examined the emotional expressions of CPS-referred children during a challenging parent–child interaction task in which children had to solve problems of increasing difficulty. Children who received the intervention showed reduced negative affect during this task, including lower expressions of anger, lower levels of anger directed at the parent, and lower levels of global anger and sadness, than children who received the control intervention. Importantly, studies have identified long-term gains in the executive function of children who received the ABC intervention. At a preschool follow-up approximately 3 years following the 10-week intervention, foster children who received the ABC intervention in infancy and toddlerhood displayed cognitive flexibility and theory of mind similar to that of typically developing children (Lewis-Morrarty et al., 2012).

In improving the parent–child relationship, an ancillary goal of the ABC intervention is to enhance psychobiological regulation among maltreated children. Findings from RCTs related to the functioning of the HPA axis among children who receive the ABC intervention suggest that it is effective in doing so. At a 1-month follow-up, Dozier and colleagues (2006) found that foster children who received the ABC intervention had patterns of diurnal cortisol regulation characteristic of typically developing children, whereas children who received the control intervention showed aberrant production. These promising findings have been extended to CPS-referred children assessed at a 1-month follow-up (Bernard, Dozier, Bick, & Gordon, 2015) and 3 years postintervention (Bernard, Hostinar, & Dozier, 2015). Bernard, Hostinar, and Dozier (2015) found that at a preschool follow-up, children who received the ABC intervention maintained a more normative pattern of diurnal cortisol regulation. As noted in Chapter 1, functioning of the HPA axis has been associated with a host of mental and physical health outcomes. Therefore, enduring improvements in cortisol production are promising for the long-term well-being of children who receive the ABC intervention.

CONCLUSION

The ABC intervention is a targeted, short-term intervention informed by research on attachment and psychobiological regulation in early life. The intervention has been implemented with maltreated children, including children in foster families and CPS-referred families. RCTs of the ABC intervention have indicated that it is effective in improving outcomes for children exposed to maltreatment in infancy and toddlerhood, a period of pronounced vulnerability to abuse and neglect. Specifically, vulnerable children who receive the intervention "catch up" to their low-risk peers, demonstrating more typical cognitive, emotional, and neurobiological functioning. Improvement in parenting behaviors, the primary goal of the ABC intervention, is the likely mechanism for resilience in these children. Importantly, both immediate and longer term gains are evident among children who receive the ABC intervention. Future research is needed to investigate maltreatment recidivism rates among parents who receive the ABC intervention.

4

Parent–Child Interaction Therapy

A s a well-established behavioral intervention for disruptive children ages 2 to 7 years, parent–child interaction therapy (PCIT) has a long-standing evidence base for addressing some of the most severe aggressive and oppositional behaviors in young children (Wagner, 2010). In the original form developed by Sheila Eyberg (1988), PCIT is appropriate for young children demonstrating externalizing and internalizing problems, severe conduct behaviors (e.g., animal cruelty, fire setting, stealing, lying), attention-deficit/hyperactivity disorder, and relational issues secondary to divorce and adoption (McNeil & Hembree-Kigin, 2010). PCIT uses in vivo parent coaching with the skills of nondirective play therapy and behavior management strategies to facilitate a two-pronged approach to improving child behaviors.

Since the initial development of PCIT for children with disruptive behaviors, clinicians and researchers in the field of child maltreatment

http://dx.doi.org/10.1037/0000030-005
Treating Infants and Young Children Impacted by Trauma: Interventions That Promote Healthy Development, by J. D. Osofsky, P. T. Stepka, and L. S. King

have applied and/or adapted the model to implement with maltreating parents (e.g., Urquiza & McNeil, 1996), maltreated children living with foster families (e.g., McNeil, Herschell, Gurwitch, & Clemens-Mowrer, 2005), and caregiver–child dyads exposed to domestic violence (e.g., Borrego, Gutow, Reicher, & Barker, 2008). Before examining the development, application, and outcomes of these efforts, it is important to review the original theory and research that established the foundation for PCIT. Following this review, we provide an overview of the original model, followed by consideration of the historical and research development of PCIT for implementation with maltreated and trauma-exposed dyads. We discuss common adaptations and considerations when using PCIT with maltreated and trauma-exposed children.

According to Patterson's (1982) coercion theory, child misbehavior is the direct result of reciprocal cycles of escalating maladaptive behaviors between parents and their children. In short, parents make a demand on their child, which the child responds to with undesired behavior (e.g., whining, defiance, aggression). In response to child misbehavior, parents either withdraw the demand (leading to increased potential for future misbehavior through negative reinforcement) or respond with escalating negative behavior of their own. Should this escalation be effective in gaining the child's compliance, parents are positively reinforced for using coercive behavior. Inconsistent responses by parents result in both parent and child maladaptive behaviors continuing and increasing through intermittent positive and negative reinforcement contingencies.

Heavily influenced by Patterson's (1982) social learning theory, the operant parent coaching models of Hanf (1969), and research findings of Baumrind (1966, 1967) on effective parenting styles, Eyberg sought to develop a parent program that strategically reversed the coercive cycle. The method used was parental coaching to develop skills that matched nurturance, positive engagement, and warmth with consistent limit setting (i.e., authoritative parenting). By teaching parents nondirective play skills, it was possible to establish (or reestablish) positive and warm child–caregiver relationships. Once a parent demonstrates mastery of these skills, it is believed that children will be more responsive to the subsequent introduction of parental commands and limit setting. As a result, the overall goal of PCIT is to reduce problematic behaviors in children by transforming less effective parenting styles (i.e., authoritarian, permissive, laissez-faire) into more positive and effective authoritative interactions.

EVIDENCE BASE FOR THE ORIGINAL PARENT–CHILD INTERACTION THERAPY MODEL

As originally designed, PCIT has been found to consistently reduce child behavior problems in multiple randomized controlled trials (e.g., Bagner & Eyberg, 2007; Boggs et al., 2005; Nixon, Sweeney, Erickson, & Touyz, 2003; Schuhmann, Foote, Eyberg, Boggs, & Algina, 1998). On follow-up, behavioral improvements have been found to persist for up to 6 years posttreatment (Hood & Eyberg, 2003), and improvements appear to generalize outside of the clinic to home (Boggs, Eyberg, & Reynolds, 1990) and school settings (McNeil, Eyberg, Hembree Eisenstadt, Newcomb, & Funderburk, 1991). Interestingly, treatment improvements have been found to generalize not only across environments but also to untreated siblings (Brestan, Eyberg, Boggs, & Algina, 1997). Compared with behavioral improvements demonstrated in the randomized controlled trials mentioned earlier, PCIT has shown similar efficacy with Spanish-speaking (McCabe, Yeh, Garland, Lau, & Chavez, 2005), Chinese-speaking (Leung, Tsang, Heung, & You, 1999), and African American families (Fernandez, Butler, & Eyberg, 2011).

Later applications of the model have found PCIT to be effective for other populations in addition to those presenting with disruptive behavior disorders. Chase and Eyberg (2008) found that the implementation of PCIT resulted in reductions in behavioral and anxiety symptoms of children with comorbid oppositional defiant disorder and separation anxiety disorder. Compared with wait-list controls, PCIT is also effective in reducing disruptive behaviors and improving parenting practices with children diagnosed with intellectual impairments and autism spectrum disorder (Bagner & Eyberg, 2007; Solomon, Ono, Timmer, & Goodlin-Jones, 2008).

SEQUENCE OF PARENT–CHILD INTERACTION THERAPY

Client Assessment Stage

From the first meeting with the caregivers to the final termination session, PCIT uses an organized and structured process. Depending on the presenting issues and number of caregivers to be involved in the course of treatment, the assessment process may range from one to several sessions. However, a typical intake with a single caregiver usually requires one to two sessions. Although a variety of information can be gained from including the child, it is strongly recommended that the initial meeting be conducted only with the caregiver. This approach gives the caregiver the freedom to fully elaborate on her or his concerns, some of which may be inappropriate or overwhelming to discuss in front of the child, and provides the clinician with the best opportunity to collect as much information as possible without unnecessary distraction. Furthermore, children referred for PCIT tend to have significant behavior problems that can be overwhelming for the caregiver and the clinician to deal with. As early as the first meeting, parents may have the expectation that clinicians, as "experts," will readily be able to manage their child's behavior and that "treatment" starts at the first contact. This unrealistic expectation can set the stage for sabotaging the caregiver's faith in the therapeutic process, and thus undermine the treatment. Finally, when working with populations exposed to trauma and abuse, meeting alone with the caregiver can allow the caregiver to talk about her or his concerns, thus facilitating an enhanced sense of confidentiality and safety.

Initial meetings with caregivers usually involve spending some time developing rapport, which is then followed by a semistructured intake interview (approximately 45 minutes) and administration of paper-and-pencil parent report measures. These often include the Eyberg Child Behavior Inventory (ECBI; Eyberg & Pincus, 1999; Eyberg & Ross, 1978), as well as the Sutter-Eyberg Student Behavior Inventory–Revised (Eyberg & Pincus, 1999; Funderburk & Eyberg, 1989) for children involved in day care or preschool. Although these preliminary details are required for all

PCIT cases to assess and monitor treatment progress, different agencies and populations will benefit from additional measures and assessments as needed. These may include a more in-depth assessment of the child's trauma history and developmental, emotional, adaptive, and cognitive abilities. Caregiver assessment in domains such as parenting stress, mental health, trauma history, and co-parenting quality may also be essential.

After this information has been gathered from the caregiver, the assessment moves to a baseline evaluation of the child–caregiver interaction. The results of these observations provide the foundation for measuring progress as well as planning treatment. The relationship is evaluated by using the Dyadic Parent–Child Interaction Coding System–IV (DPICS-IV; Eyberg, Chase, Fernandez, & Nelson, 2014). The DPICS-IV involves three sequential 5-minute observation periods: (a) child-led play, (b) parent-led play, and (c) cleanup. The parent and child are provided with a comfortably spaced room that includes a workspace area (with age-appropriate chairs and table), a time-out chair in the corner, five sets of toys (e.g., LEGOs, dolls, blocks, puzzles, animals) distributed on the workspace and around the floor, and a central container for cleanup. In child-led play, the parent is directed to simply follow the child's lead during the play and allow the latter to play in any way he or she desires. Conversely, during parent-led play, the parent is directed to take over the play with the same materials. In this condition, the expectation is that the child will follow the parent's rules and that the caregiver will enforce these requirements using his or her typical style. Finally, during cleanup, the parent is directed to command the child to clean up, with the expectation that the child will put all the toys away by him- or herself. Across all three conditions, the clinician observes this process (usually through a two-way mirror) while measuring child and parent behaviors with the DPICS-IV coding system. The parent's behaviors and responses are measured in nine behavioral categories: use of specific labeled praise, reflection of the child's talk, verbal description of the child's behavior, "neutral talk" (i.e., parent verbalizations that are neither evaluative nor descriptive about the child's actions), unlabeled praise, direct or specific commands, indirect or nonspecific commands, questions, and "negative talk" (e.g., criticism, sarcasm). Similarly, child behavior is coded for compliance or non-compliance in response to parental commands.

When the intake information and observations have been collected and analyzed, the caregiver is provided with feedback on the clinician's impressions of the child as well as a description of and orientation to PCIT. This feedback session includes further joining with the parent, giving an explanation and rationale for dyadic treatment, contracting around attendance and homework expectations, and scheduling of sessions. Before the end of the final feedback meeting, the parent is given her or his first "homework assignment." She or he is asked to begin tracking the child's behavior daily and finding time to spend with the child one-on-one for approximately five minutes each day. For the remainder of treatment, this documentation, along with the newly completed ECBIs, will be reviewed with the parent at the beginning of each session to keep consistent track of the child's behavioral improvements and the parent's participation in treatment and to resolve any emergent concerns with the caregiver.

Consistent with other early childhood treatments, PCIT is a dyadic model. The individual parent–child dyad is considered a unique unit of treatment. As a result, when multiple caregivers are involved in PCIT, separate assessment processes are completed for each child–caregiver dyad. In treatment, both parents may attend sessions, but the actual work of child-directed interaction and parent-directed interaction focuses on only one parent and one child at a time. Multiple caregivers are included in treatment in various ways. For instance, in intact parent families, both parents may attend 90-minute treatment sessions, but the actual parent–child interaction will be split between the parents (e.g., 45 minutes of mother and child followed by 45 minutes of father and child). Similarly, different caregivers may attend treatment on rotating weeks, or if tolerated by the family, multiple weekly sessions may be scheduled.

Treatment Stages

An overview of the stages of PCIT appears in Table 4.1. The treatment phase of PCIT comprises two main sequential stages. Child-directed interaction is the first phase, followed by parent-directed interaction. In

Table 4.1

Overview of Parent–Child Interaction Therapy by Stage

Stage	Session content
Self-motivation enhancement (6 sessions)	*Participant testimonials, pro and con balance exercises on use of physical discipline and change, development of parenting and relationship goals, discussion of reality and goal discrepancy, and encouragement to commit to change*
Assessment (1–2 sessions)	Pretreatment assessment including semi-structured interview, ECBI, DPICS-IV, broadband measures (e.g., BASC-2/CBCL), and presenting-issues specific assessments (e.g., *trauma screening*, parental functioning)
CDI orientation	Feedback and parent-only instruction on CDI skills (60–90 minutes), *orientation to post-traumatic play and emotional attunement*
CDI coaching (4–6 sessions)	5 to 10 minute review of progress and parental concerns, 5-minute observation of child–parent interaction followed by in vivo coaching of CDI skills (30–40 minutes), *provision of trauma and developmentally informed reframes of child misbehavior (if applicable) and post-traumatic play*
PDI orientation	Parent-only instruction on PDI skills (60–90 minutes) *Orientation to parental emotion monitoring and emotion regulation strategies*
PDI coaching (4–6 sessions)	5 to 10 minute review of progress and parental concerns, 5-minute observation of child–parent interaction followed by in vivo coaching of PDI skills (30–40 minutes)
Termination (1–2 sessions)	Post-treatment assessment (e.g., re-administration of intake measures and DPICS-IV), *and graduation session with family*
Follow-up	Booster sessions as needed

Note. Components in italics represent modifications to the traditional parent–child interaction therapy protocol for work with maltreated children and abusive caregivers. BASC-2/CBCL = Behavior Assessment System for Children, Second Edition/Achenbach Child Behavior Checklist; CDI = child-directed interaction; DPICS-IV = Dyadic Parent–Child Interaction Coding System–IV; ECBI = Eyberg Child Behavior Inventory; PDI = parent-directed interaction. Data from Chaffin et al. (2009), McNeil and Hembree-Kigin (2010), and UC Davis Children's Hospital (2016).

child-directed interaction (CDI) the parent is taught the skills of nondirective play therapy. These skills are broken down into what are called the *PRIDE skills*: praise, reflection, imitation, description, and enthusiasm. In short, the caregiver is taught to provide specific rather than nonspecific or vague praise for desired behaviors, reflect or paraphrase the child's verbalizations, imitate and copy the child's actions in play, provide regular verbal descriptions of the child's actions, and most important, bring a sense of enjoyment and energy into the play interactions with the child. CDI begins with a parent-only coaching session in which each of the skills is described, modeled, and practiced before implementing them in vivo with the child. Furthermore, as parents may be skeptical about playing with their misbehaving children, the theoretical and empirical rationale for each skill is provided, and parents have an opportunity to address their doubts and concerns. In contrast, parents are also warned about the "DON'T" behaviors. These are the behaviors that the therapist encourages parents to minimize during CDI. The DON'Ts include questions, critical or sarcastic talk, and commands. Similarly, the skill of "active ignoring" in response to nondangerous misbehavior during CDI sessions is also reviewed and modeled for the caregiver.

After the parent has demonstrated cognitive understanding of the PRIDE, DON'T, and active ignoring skills, live coaching sessions begin. Live sessions typically consist of a brief check-in with the parent during which homework is reviewed, concerns are briefly addressed, and the current skills to be practiced are described and modeled. The therapist then exits and provides coaching while observing the dyad through a mirror or closed-circuit video system using a "bug-in-ear" communication device. Initially, clinicians focus on only developing one or two PRIDE skills at a time. To further enhance the caregiver's acquisition of skills, they are encouraged to practice CDI daily with their child, document these "special play times," and process their experiences by practicing with the therapist at the beginning of each session. As parents demonstrate more proficiency, they are expected to achieve mastery of all PRIDE skills before being allowed to "graduate" to the parent-directed interaction stage of PCIT. Mastery criteria are clearly described to caregivers before commencing CDI, and the treatment progress of caregivers is regularly reviewed at the beginning and ending of each CDI session.

Like CDI, the initial *parent-directed interaction* (PDI) session is also done only with the caregiver. In PDI the parent is taught behavioral strategies to increase child compliance with parental commands while reducing the frequency and intensity of maladaptive behavioral outbursts. PDI skills include the use of developmentally appropriate, concise, and specific commands; differential reinforcement and punishment (i.e., praising compliance, ignoring attention-seeking misbehavior, and enforcing predetermined consequences for noncompliance); calm use of time-out procedures; and the development of regular house rules and expectations. Once the skills have been reviewed and modeled with the caregiver, in vivo coaching sessions recommence in the same format as the CDI (i.e., therapist gradually moving from demonstration and modeling to out-of-room telecoaching). PCIT sessions from this point forward are a combination of CDI episodes followed by brief PDI practice. Termination of PCIT is considered once parents have demonstrated sufficient mastery and use of both CDI and PDI skills as well as measurable reductions in their child's initial presenting behaviors. For a more thorough description of the assessment and treatment stages of PCIT, the reader is directed to McNeil and Hembree-Kigin (2010).

APPLICATION TO TRAUMA-EXPOSED CHILDREN AND DEVELOPING EMPIRICAL SUPPORT

Unlike the other models described in this volume (child–parent psychotherapy and the attachment and biobehavioral catch-up intervention) PCIT was not originally developed with a focus on trauma or maltreatment, nor does it specifically target trauma symptoms. However, considering the frequent appearance of behavior problems in traumatized children, as well as the reciprocal nature of parent–child interactions in initiating and maintaining abuse cycles, clinicians and researchers began experimenting with and adapting PCIT to help children and their families in other stressful and traumatic contexts (Ware & Herschell, 2010). Three such areas are working with physically abusive caregivers, foster caregivers, and dyads exposed to domestic violence.

Parent–Child Interaction Therapy for Children
Exposed to Physical Abuse

As discussed previously, PCIT's origins have a strong foundation in Patterson's (1982) model of coercive relationships. Urquiza and McNeil (1996) logically expanded this model to illustrate the possible perpetuating factors of child physical abuse. They posited that not only does the coercive cycle lead to and maintain disruptive behavior problems in children, it can also lead to the development of physically abusive behaviors by parents with predisposing risk factors (e.g., previous trauma, substance abuse, environmental hardship). Contemporary researchers and clinicians have confirmed these early observations and hypotheses. Proximal factors that appear to mediate parents' physically abusive behaviors include increased negative interactions with their children paired with disengagement during positive or neutral interactions (Cicchetti & Valentino, 2006; Wilson, Rack, Shi, & Norris, 2008). On the basis of these early hypotheses, Urquiza and other clinicians proposed that the same factors that improve the parent–child relationship in the context of PCIT could also lead to reduced recidivism of child physical abuse in maltreating dyads (Chaffin et al., 2004; Hakman, Chaffin, Funderburk, & Silovsky, 2009).

Unlike traditional applications of PCIT emphasizing child behavior problems, PCIT with physically abusive parents emphasizes the "reduction of harsh, violent, or neglectful parenting practices" over changes in child behaviors (Chaffin et al., 2004, p. 84). PCIT has demonstrated the ability to reverse these patterns quickly and maintain such gains throughout treatment stages (Hakman et al., 2009). In randomized controlled and clinical comparison studies, changes in these hypothesized mediators have been associated with reduced abuse recidivism rates in parents participating in PCIT (Chaffin et al., 2004, 2009; Chaffin, Funderburk, Bard, Valle, & Gurwitch, 2011; Lanier, Kohl, Benz, Swinger, & Drake, 2014; Thomas & Zimmer-Gembeck, 2011; Timmer, Urquiza, Zebell, & McGrath, 2005). Treatment using PCIT demonstrated similar reductions in negative behaviors of maltreated children with disruptive behavior problems regardless of whether the participating caregiver was a perpetrator of abuse or a nonoffending caregiver (Timmer et al., 2005). Furthermore, like the reductions in disruptive behaviors shown in traditional PCIT cases, acting-out children with identified maltreatment histories demonstrated similar reductions in behaviors and symptoms when compared with a nonabused comparison group (Timmer et al., 2005).

Although these initial findings are encouraging, some of the greatest reductions in physical abuse recidivism were demonstrated in experimental settings (e.g., Chaffin et al., 2004). Findings also indicated that substantial reductions in efficacy and retention in treatment have negatively affected the application of PCIT to typical treatment settings such as community-based clinics (Chaffin et al., 2011; Lanier et al., 2014). Several factors have been identified that lead to decreased efficacy and retention. Lanier and colleagues (2014) found that parents who had a history of being abused as children and a history of perpetrating child abuse were 20 times more likely to abuse their children again, despite participating in PCIT, compared with caregivers without similar histories. Caregivers who did not have daily access to their children had poorer outcomes than a comparison group with children living in the home (Chaffin et al., 2011), highlighting the limitations of using PCIT with families with protective orders and mandates for supervised visitation. Families who reported children with the most severe behavior problems at intake were most likely to drop out early (Timmer et al., 2005). As Urquiza and McNeil (1996) suggested in their initial call to apply PCIT to maltreating dyads, enhancing engagement and caregiver motivation and implementing PCIT in realistic settings are likely necessary ingredients for maintaining the effectiveness of PCIT outcomes.

In response to the potential limitations and observed setbacks in applying PCIT to work with families in the child welfare system, Chaffin and colleagues (2004, 2009, 2011) used an additional adjunctive six-session self-motivational enhancement module (SM) based on W. R. Miller and Rollnick's (1991) motivational interviewing strategies. This adapted model was found to increase retention of child welfare–involved families to 85% with SM plus PCIT, versus an average of 61% for other models (including PCIT without an SM component; Chaffin et al., 2009). Especially encouraging was the finding that the SM plus PCIT was most effective at retaining families with the lowest measured motivation at intake. Further, when the SM plus PCIT adaptation was applied in real-world settings (i.e., community clinics with high referrals from child welfare agencies), abuse recidivism was reduced to 29% versus 47% when compared with treatment as usual conditions (with and without SM) and traditional applications of PCIT without SM (Chaffin et al., 2011).

Interestingly, with regard to treatment dose and parental mastery of CDI skills, Thomas and Zimmer-Gembeck (2012) found that using a standard 12-session PCIT protocol (four to six sessions of CDI followed by four to six PDI sessions) and moving forward with PDI regardless of parental mastery of CDI skills was found to have equal outcomes regarding behavioral improvements, reduced parenting stress, and measured abuse potential compared with open-ended treatment (i.e., waiting for parental mastery of CDI skills before moving to PDI and postponing termination until PDI skills and child behaviors reach desired levels). Overall, these findings lead to the conclusion that enhancing motivation paired with a concrete completion time and relatively quick progression to the PDI stage are all indicated in enhancing engagement and commitment and reducing future abuse in dyads with a history of maltreatment.

Parent–Child Interaction Therapy for Children Exposed to Domestic Violence

Like Urquiza and McNeil's (1996) call for the application of PCIT to maltreating dyads, Borrego et al. (2008) brought attention to the potential benefits of PCIT for children exposed to domestic violence. Borrego and colleagues noted that children exposed to domestic violence often develop severe behavior problems, and understandably, their abused caregivers are under extreme stress. The combination of these two factors can lead to intense negativity and maladaptive interactions among domestic violence–exposed dyads. Preliminary attempts to apply PCIT to dyads exposed to domestic violence are promising. In a study of 62 parent–child dyads exposed to domestic violence, children demonstrated substantial reductions in behavior problems, and domestic violence-exposed dyads were retained in treatment at similar levels to community referrals without a history of domestic violence (Timmer, Ware, Urquiza, & Zebell, 2010).

However, although PCIT was associated with reductions in parenting stress and parent–child relationship problems, caregivers showed no change in overall levels of distress (e.g., social, financial, emotional problems). Like the findings of Lanier and colleagues (2014) regarding caregivers with prior histories of trauma, PCIT appeared to have a positive impact on the parent–child relationship, yet caregivers continued to remain troubled by their posttraumatic experiences and other life stressors.

Parent–Child Interaction Therapy for Children in Foster Care

Children in the foster care system are exposed to many stressful experiences and have experienced multiple losses and relationship disruptions. Therefore, it is important to know to what degree PCIT maintains its robust efficacy when working with temporary and/or transitional caregivers. McNeil et al. (2005) argued that foster parent stress associated with caring for disruptive children may lead to burnout, failed placements, and negative caregiver–child interactions. These concerns led the group to develop a brief training model to support foster caregivers in their efforts to care for abused and displaced children who often present with extremely challenging (e.g., aggressive and sexualized) behaviors. McNeil and colleagues described a 2-day workshop for foster parents that highlighted the development of CDI and PDI skills. Although this model did not use in vivo coaching, reports from participants indicated high satisfaction, and child behaviors were reduced below clinical cutoffs at 5-month follow-ups. In more traditional applications of PCIT, treatment is just as effective with foster parents as biological parents, and both foster and biological parents were more likely to complete PCIT if the child in their care had been exposed to abuse (Timmer, Urquiza, & Zebell, 2006). Like Thomas and Zimmer-Gembeck's (2012) findings with physical abuse, brief protocols appear to be just as effective as extended protocols with foster caregivers (Chaffin et al., 2004). With regard to foster parent well-being and efficacy, PCIT resulted in a reduction in parenting stress as well as improvement of observed parenting behavior (Mersky, Topitzes, Janczewski, & McNeil, 2015).

Adaptations and Considerations in the Use of Parent–Child Interaction Therapy With Trauma-Exposed Children

Although the original PCIT model can stand alone as a robust and effective treatment for improving a wide range of disruptive behaviors and negative parent–child interactions, applying PCIT as a one-size-fits-all approach with trauma-exposed children is contraindicated. From the initial contact with the caregiver to the final termination session, there are several important considerations and modifications to consider in applying PCIT principles to abuse and trauma-exposed children and their caregivers. The following recommendations are either direct suggestions from existing PCIT protocols for trauma-exposed children or inferred from the existing literature (Chaffin et al., 2004; UC Davis Children's Hospital, 2016; Urquiza & Timmer, 2014; Ware & Herschell, 2010).

ASSESSMENT IN PARENT–CHILD INTERACTION THERAPY

Considering the significant impact of caregiver history of trauma on recidivism and retention outcomes, it is highly recommended that clinicians assess both a caregiver's trauma history as well as current symptoms of posttraumatic stress. Similarly, knowledge of the child's exposure to traumatic experiences, situational triggers, and trauma symptoms further guides the clinician in treatment planning as well as appropriate referrals if needed. Although caregivers report improvements in parent–child relationships and decreased parenting stress following PCIT, the extant literature indicates overall distress remains unchanged in caregivers exposed to trauma. It may be beneficial to provide distressed caregivers with outside referrals to address issues not adequately helped by PCIT.

During the initial intake interview, it is important for clinicians to inquire about the family's current case plan as well as any restrictions on child access between sessions. As discussed earlier, parents who have regular access to their children engage longer and improve more during treatment compared with caregivers whose children live outside the home. Disruptive child behaviors can be extremely overwhelming for caregivers.

Therefore, it would also be useful to assess caregivers' current emotional reactions to child misbehavior to provide a better understanding of their emotional coping strategies. A common component of maltreatment-focused PCIT is developing and enhancing caregivers' emotion regulation capacities, most often to help them actively ignore child misbehavior and implement discipline strategies in a calm manner. In addition to emotional safety, it is essential for the clinician to have assessed the current level of safety in the home. It is unrealistic to expect either the caregiver or the child to make substantial improvements if between sessions they are continually exposed to dangerous environments. Although not physically dangerous, placement stability is also a safety concern. When working with foster caregivers, it will be useful to know to what degree the placement is stable as well as current plans for reunification and/or permanent placement or adoption.

CHILD-DIRECTED INTERACTION IN PARENT–CHILD INTERACTION THERAPY

The core feature of CDI is play. Although aggressive and frightening play is actively discouraged and ignored in the standard PCIT protocol, this variety of play is likely to emerge when working with traumatized children and requires a qualitatively different response. According to the trauma team at UC Davis (UC Davis Children's Hospital, 2016), posttraumatic play should be anticipated, and psychoeducation should be provided to parents to better prepare them should it arise. Clinicians should be ready to calm and regulate the caregiver (e.g., using breathing skills, counting to 10) because observing such play in their children can be overwhelming. Once caregivers are regulated, the clinician can walk them through the steps of following their child's lead and attempting to move their play to a safe resolution.

Parents with a history of abusive behaviors may require additional practice in administering specific praise and recognizing their child's positive behaviors. Urquiza and Timmer (2014) noted that parents' negative cognitions about their children and interpretations of their behavior can be so entrenched that therapists may have to provide unstructured developmental guidance in the moment if they observe parents having intense or negative reactions to developmentally appropriate behavior.

Such reframing may have to be frequent and well timed to effectively reverse parents' attentional biases toward child misbehavior and negative responses to developmentally appropriate behavior.

PARENT-DIRECTED INTERACTION IN PARENT–CHILD INTERACTION THERAPY

Several modifications to the PDI protocol are needed when working with abused and maltreated children. Although older and more traditional PCIT protocols advocated mild corporal punishment and physical holding when children refused time out, "hands off" approaches are considered standard for PDI with maltreated children and are found to be equally as effective as more aggressive approaches (Chaffin et al., 2004, 2011; Urquiza & Timmer, 2014). Common examples include removal of all toys, time-out rooms, and response cost strategies to encourage compliance with PDI discipline strategies.

Preparation and providing children with the rationale for parenting commands is not commonly emphasized in traditional PCIT protocols. However, considering the level of emotional lability and dysregulation demonstrated by maltreated children, caregivers are encouraged to provide as much predictability, structure, and explanation as possible before implementing discipline strategies. Similarly, to enhance understanding and predictability, children are often used as cotherapists in the development and practice of discipline strategies and punishments. For instance, children may be coached in the use of time-out with dolls or stuffed animals and then encouraged to role play this process with their caregivers. This provides a clear picture of response contingencies for misbehavior and more opportunities for parents to practice time-out without having to engage directly in negative interactions with their children.

TERMINATION IN PARENT–CHILD INTERACTION THERAPY

Finally, as families begin to approach the end of treatment, children and parents may become anxious or triggered because ending may serve as a reminder of prior losses or traumas. Conversely, mandated caregivers may be anxious about open-ended treatments with vague completion requirements. As noted in Thomas and Zimmer-Gembeck's study (2012), parents involved in child welfare maintained better retention in shorter, well-defined PCIT protocols that moved rapidly from CDI to PDI. Thomas and Zimmer-Gembeck hypothesized that mandated parents are possibly more likely to complete treatments with a distinct beginning, middle, and end. Furthermore, parents with difficult children are often anxious to learn discipline strategies sooner rather than later and struggle with the mastery requirements of CDI before being allowed to learn discipline strategies. Like their children, parents may benefit from the enhanced structure and predictability of shorter and explicitly scheduled treatment plans.

Having completed a thorough trauma screen and collected caregiving background history during the assessment stage, the clinician should be alert and prepared for possible reactions the family may have as the final session approaches. Special care should be taken in terminating treatment with children and parents who have significant histories of loss, death, abandonment, and other major relationship ruptures. Children who have been abused and/or in foster care may have endured many negative transitions and may not see "graduation" through the same lens of accomplishment and achievement as the therapist or other adults. Therefore, it is important for the therapist to consider ways to talk openly with the family about treatment ending, but in a way that is still consistent with PCIT. This may involve keeping a visual schedule of treatment sessions that remain, providing parents with copies of old treatment documentation, and saving examples of work products completed throughout treatment (especially artwork and pictures taken during CDI) to be shared and reflected on during the final sessions.

CONCLUSION

Although the preliminary evidence of the efficacy of PCIT for the prevention of future abuse and reduction of externalizing difficulties in traumatized children is encouraging, clinicians and researchers have nonetheless noted limitations and the need for cautions. In working with perpetrators of child maltreatment, PCIT is emerging as a promising intervention in preventing future physical abuse of young children. However, this treatment approach is still strongly contraindicated for use with sexually abusive parents (California Evidence-Based Clearinghouse for Child Welfare, 2016; Chadwick Center on Children and Families, 2004; Lanier et al., 2014; Ware & Herschell, 2010) and has limited efficacy with neglecting caregivers (Chaffin et al., 2004). Considering that neglect accounts for over 75% of maltreatment cases (Child Welfare Information Gateway, 2015), ways that PCIT can be modified to better address and reduce issues of neglect are worthy of future investigation.

For children diagnosed with posttraumatic stress disorder (PTSD), it should be noted that PCIT does not directly target trauma symptoms such as avoidance, hyperarousal, and posttraumatic reexperiencing (Borrego et al., 2008). However, it could be argued that many of the behavioral difficulties demonstrated by maltreated children are, in fact, expressions of posttraumatic stress and that PCIT indirectly treats trauma by reestablishing safety, improving attachment relationships, and creating new environments to address posttraumatic triggering (Urquiza & Timmer, 2014). Nonetheless, to date, there are no published studies supporting the use of PCIT in reducing symptoms of PTSD.

Despite these limitations and cautions, PCIT has been shown to be an effective treatment that clinicians may use in working with young children exposed to maltreatment. The strongest evidence for PCIT in the field of maltreatment is in preventing future physical abuse. The effectiveness of PCIT is further enhanced by motivational self-enhancement strategies and attention to the collateral impacts of caregiver trauma on treatment outcomes and retention. Unlike standard PCIT, abuse-focused PCIT targets caregiver behaviors as a primary domain of change and safety enhancement. It has been found to be equally effective with physically abusive parents, nonoffending caregivers, and foster parents. Although current applications of PCIT in the field of maltreatment emphasize parental improvements and stress reduction, abuse-focused PCIT continues to maintain behavioral improvements in children at similar levels to the original model and application.

5

Considerations in Choosing a Treatment That Works

In the previous chapters, we described three evidence-based treatments designed to help young children and their families affected by trauma, including child–parent psychotherapy (CPP), attachment and biobehavioral catch-up (ABC), and parent–child interaction therapy (PCIT). All of these treatments work through the parent–child relationship to help the child recover and resume a positive developmental trajectory, while also supporting the parent and healing the parent–child relationship.

The goal of this chapter is to assist the clinician in deciding which treatment approach is most helpful when addressing a specific behavioral problem, relational issue, or both. To assist the reader in comparing and contrasting approaches, Table 5.1 provides side-by-side descriptions of each treatment. We also outline criteria relevant to choosing a treatment that works. This method for helping the clinician decide which treatment "might work for whom" has been used in previous guides for clinical work

http://dx.doi.org/10.1037/0000030-006
Treating Infants and Young Children Impacted by Trauma: Interventions That Promote Healthy Development, by J. D. Osofsky, P. T. Stepka, and L. S. King
Copyright © 2017 by the American Psychological Association. All rights reserved.

Table 5.1

Comparison of Treatments for Trauma-Exposed Young Children

	CPP	ABC	PCIT
Main theoretical background	Psychodynamic; attachment theory[a,b]	Attachment theory[a,b]	Parenting styles,[c] operant parent coaching models,[d] attachment theory,[b] coercion theory[e]
Major treatment goals	Achieving secure attachment	Decreasing risk for disorganized attachment	Increasing authoritative parenting
	Constructing a joint trauma narrative; decreasing child and parent PTS symptoms	Increasing parental synchrony and nurturance; decreasing intrusive and frightening behavior	Increasing parental warmth, non-directive play, and limit setting
	Improving emotion and behavior regulation	Enhancing child psychobiological regulation	Reducing child disruptive behavior
Inclusion criteria	Ages 0–6 years	Ages 6–24 months	Ages 2–7 years
	Exposed to all types of trauma	Exposed to maltreatment	Exposed to physical or emotional abuse, or domestic violence
			Child disruptive behavior
Exclusion criteria[f]	Parent unwilling to participate	Parent unwilling to participate	Parent unwilling to participate
			Child moderate to severe PTS
Duration	50 60-minute weekly sessions	10 60-minute weekly sessions	12–20 60-minute weekly sessions
Setting	Clinic or home	Home	Clinic

Note. ABC = attachment and biobehavioral catch-up; CPP = child–parent psychotherapy; PCIT = parent–child interaction therapy; PTS = posttraumatic stress.
[a]Bowlby (1988). [b]Ainsworth (1989). [c]Baumrind (1966). [d]Hanf (1969). [e]Patterson (1982). [f]For all dyadic treatments, immediate safety should be established first and treatment cannot involve a caregiver who has perpetrated sexual abuse. Furthermore, parents with severe developmental disorders or mental illness (e.g., schizophrenia) or active substance abuse may be unable to participate in treatments.

with older children and adolescents (Fonagy et al., 2014). The guide presented in this chapter, specific for work with young children, will also be helpful for agencies that are considering training for clinicians in a specific evidence-based treatment.

From a training perspective, it is often difficult to help students decide which treatment is most appropriate for a population or an individual and might best address the presenting problem or traumatic experience. Education for undergraduate and graduate students on clinical interventions and treatments for young children and families should ideally include classes and didactic training in various interventions and treatments and, if possible, offer opportunities to learn and practice the different treatment approaches at the experiential level. Realistically, however, most training programs have a specific theoretical orientation and teach students treatment approaches that are based on that perspective. Although students may enter the program with an open mind, most leave their training programs with knowledge and experiences specific to a particular theoretical orientation. The experiences that trainees and clinicians receive in their various educational settings and training programs influence their choice of treatments.

The three evidence-based treatments for young children and their families require intensive training that varies in length from 1 year to 18 months. Being trained to implement these treatments requires both in-person training, ranging from one to three sessions in 18 months, and telephone consultation calls ranging from two to four a month. In addition, trainees have to provide treatment for a certain number of cases, depending on the treatment approach, with consistent regularly scheduled consultation and case presentations during the training. Information about training and access to training manuals for each of the three treatments is available online (CPP: http://childtrauma.ucsf.edu/child-parent-psychotherapy-training; ABC: http://www.infantcaregiverproject.com; PCIT: http://pcit.ucdavis.edu). In this chapter, we provide information and viewpoints that are important in decision making related to treatment approaches for young children, especially those exposed to trauma.

As detailed in Table 5.1, the theoretical frameworks for CPP, ABC, and PCIT include psychodynamic, attachment, and social learning theory. The theoretical orientation of the clinician certainly plays a role in the treatment chosen to address behavioral, emotional, and relational issues in young children. Whichever treatment is used, the goal is to help the child return to a positive developmental trajectory. Central to the success of the therapeutic work is supporting the strengths in both the child and the caregiver(s). Additional goals of treatment for the clinician may determine the choice of intervention strategy, including issues as basic as the length of time the clinicians and the family are willing and able to commit to treatment. Further, the philosophy of the clinician or the agency where he or she works may contraindicate one or more of the treatment approaches for a particular case. It is always important to recognize therapist factors that can influence not just the choice but also the course of treatment. To implement any of these treatments effectively, therapists should be aware of their biases and the ways they prefer to work with young children and families. For example, ABC works with families in the home. Many CPP clinicians are clinic based; however, CPP is also delivered in homes. PCIT is done in a clinic setting.

Attention to the cultural values of families is also important in building the therapeutic relationship and guiding treatment. By understanding each family according to their unique cultural background, their values can be respected and the therapeutic work tailored to be as consistent as possible with those values. A trusting relationship with families can be built more effectively if cultural customs and ways of relating are understood. In considering the effects of trauma on young children, it is also crucial to understand contextual issues, including poverty, minority status, and other familial factors that, if not sensitively addressed, can contribute to resistance to initiating treatment or possibly premature termination of treatment. The overall result, unfortunately, is often continuing disparities in care. For example, poverty may pose basic challenges to receiving treatment, such as problems in arranging transportation to appointments, as well as more complex challenges, such as more frequent exposure to community stressors.

In addition to the descriptions presented in Table 5.1, we provide side-by-side descriptions of CPP, ABC, and PCIT in Figure 5.1, which presents a step model to help guide clinicians in decision making about which treatment to use for different infant and young child cases. To further assist

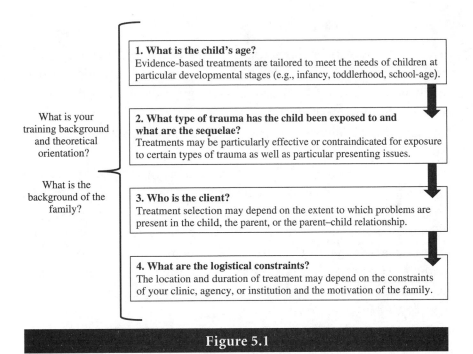

Figure 5.1

Considerations in selecting a treatment that works.

the reader, we describe several cases to help elucidate the decision-making process of selecting a treatment to use, including the reasons behind each treatment decision. The illustrative cases should be helpful to clinicians new to the field and those with more experience. This section may also provide guidance to aid in administrative decisions related to training clinicians and selecting treatments for young traumatized children.

TREATMENT SELECTION FRAMEWORK

Criterion 1: Age

One of the most straightforward indicators for treatment selection is age. Although CPP is appropriate from infancy through early childhood (ages 0–6 years), ABC is best suited for infants and toddlers (ages 6–24 months), and PCIT for toddlers and older children (ages 2–7 years).

Criterion 2: Traumatic Exposure

The second decision for the clinician involves the nature of the child's traumatic exposure. Considering that all three treatments use a relational (most often dyadic) framework, the clinician must consider whether the trauma was interpersonal in nature and, if so, in what ways the trauma involved the caregiver. Originally, CPP focused on the treatment of young children and their mothers exposed to domestic violence (Lieberman, Ghosh Ippen, & Van Horn, 2015). Therefore, traumas that are coexperienced by the caregiver and child, or witnessed by the child but not directly perpetrated by the caregiver, indicate selecting CPP. Conversely, in instances in which the caregiver who will be actively involved in treatment has also engaged in abusive or frightening behavior toward the child, ABC or PCIT, both of which have a direct emphasis on replacing pathogenic caregiving with sensitive caregiving, may be the most appropriate interventions.

Criterion 3: Sequelae of Traumatic Exposure

In addition to considering the type of traumatic exposure, the clinician has to determine how to conceptualize the presenting issues of the case. Do the child's presenting issues involve symptoms of posttraumatic stress disorder (PTSD), disruptive behavior, parental insensitivity and responsiveness, and/or other developmental, medical, and neurological issues? Considering that CPP is the only intervention that specifically targets symptoms of PTSD and describes an articulated strategy for responding to posttraumatic reexperiencing (e.g., posttraumatic play and behavioral reenactments), it may be the best choice for children who present with posttraumatic stress symptoms. However, in cases in which it is less clear that the child's behavioral and emotional disturbance is a direct response to intrusive recollections and feelings, it is important for the caregiver to have specific guidance in dealing with the child's changing affective states and building her or his sense of security and autonomy. For these cases, the accessible, discrete, and structured nature of ABC may be most appropriate. When children are also disruptive and parents need concrete behavior management skills, PCIT may be the best choice.

Criterion 4: Who Is the Client?

From a procedural coding and managed care perspective, dyadic treatments may pose a dilemma. Not infrequently, when clinicians are first referred a case, especially if the referral source is involved with child welfare, it may be unclear as to whether it is the parent, the child, or the relationship that is the designated "patient." Although a discussion of the accurate procedural codes to use when billing for any of these treatments is outside the scope of this volume, it is important that the clinician consider this question in deciding what treatment may be the best choice. For instance, in cases in which maltreatment is the presenting issue and the involved caregiver has played a significant role as a perpetrator of the maltreatment, the treatments of choice may be ABC or PCIT, both of which emphasize assessing and working to directly change caregiver behavior. Similarly, in cases in which there are clearly reciprocal escalating coercive behaviors between the parent and the child, PCIT would likely be most helpful in interrupting the negative interaction patterns. However, if the caregiver's difficulty in appropriately and effectively responding to his or her child is influenced by his or her history of trauma or pathogenic caregiving (i.e., "ghosts in the nursery"), CPP may be the more appropriate choice, with greater emphasis on improving caregiver mental health, internal representations, and well-being. Further, like ABC, CPP uses strategies for enhancing the caregiver's understanding of the child's behavior and emotional needs. CPP not only enhances understanding and increases the caregiver's responsiveness, but also helps make meaning of the experiences for the child. This type of treatment intervention helps the child feels less overwhelmed and more able to develop her or his self-regulatory capacities.

Criterion 5: Caregivers' Capacity to Participate, Retention, and Duration of Access

Finally, the clinician must consider three practical issues before deciding on and commencing treatment: (a) whether there are any contraindications in beginning treatment with the available caregiver; (b) how likely it is that the family will remain in treatment; and (c) if they do participate, the limitations to their access to services. Clinical sites vary widely in both their referral sources and agency policies regarding number of sessions offered. At times, inappropriate referrals are made by well-meaning, yet poorly informed, sources when caregiver participation may further endanger the child or caregiver. Although some clinics may primarily work with self-referred, highly motivated families and have the opportunity to provide mainly open-ended treatment, referrals from other agencies may be court mandated. For example, for children in the child welfare system who are under the supervision of the court, time limitations may be imposed on the duration of treatment because of the Adoption and Safe Families Act of 1997, which states that children's health and safety must be the paramount concern. In these cases, a major goal of treatment is to move children who are in foster care under the supervision of the court into permanent homes with the biological parent, a relative, or an adoptive parent as quickly as possible.

In addition to the issue of not working with perpetrators of sexual abuse, other caregiver issues may contraindicate relationship-focused treatments. Caregivers with severe mental illness that is untreated and/or those who are actively abusing substances should have these conditions addressed before commencing any of the interventions highlighted in this volume. In situations in which client motivation is low, or the client is unable to reach the clinic, ABC, which is home based, may be more effective. In addition, PCIT protocols with adjunct self-motivation modules might be highly beneficial when client motivation is low. Both ABC and PCIT have relatively brief and structured treatment approaches, with distinct stages and endpoints, which may facilitate client retention. In contrast, CPP would be appropriate for individuals and settings that were more flexible in length of treatment. CPP can reach a broader range of presenting issues, including complex and intergenerational trauma as well as mental health issues in the parent influencing both parent and child outcomes.

CASE ILLUSTRATIONS[1]

Case 1

Emily, age 2 years, was referred by Child Protective Services (CPS) after a neighbor found her wandering on the street alone. The second time

---

[1] Case examples have been disguised to protect patient confidentiality.

the neighbor saw the child, she called the police. Although CPS was following the case, the agency did not place Emily in foster care because her grandmother, who also lived in the home with her mother, Mary, agreed to watch the child more carefully. Emily's mother, Mary, age 21 years, was depressed, had diabetes and high blood pressure, and spent most of her time in bed. Mary was raised by her grandmother, who was also depressed and intermittently abused drugs. Although Emily's grandmother was able to provide physical care, she could not give Emily the nurturance and emotional support that are so important for young children. Mary felt too exhausted much of the time to care for Emily. She had never learned "good enough" parenting as a child.

Emily's father was the victim of physical abuse and neglect at the hands of both his mother and stepfather. He spent his adolescence in foster care. He had no contact with his birth family or foster family and was only able to find temporary construction jobs, which provided some income for the family. His violent temper and abuse of alcohol contributed to domestic violence, which led to his arrest. Without Emily's father, the family was in a difficult financial situation. Emily missed her father a lot because, when he was sober, he liked to play with her and take her outside. He was more emotionally available to her than her depressed mother. However, whenever she mentioned missing Daddy, Mary became upset, so Emily withdrew and played by herself. Emily withdrew from her caregivers often, while at other times she screamed and cried when her mother left to go to her intermittent cleaning jobs. Given that there was little supervision, Emily learned how to push open the unlocked door of their home and wander into the street. Adding to Mary's worries, Emily's grandmother was aging and ill, and Mary feared she would be unable to help care for Emily before too long. Mary wanted Emily to have a better life than she had but, unfortunately, was too depressed most of the time to recognize she must play with Emily and be emotionally available. She applied to Early Head Start for Emily, hoping that Emily would be able to have a good start in learning.

Before Emily was found wandering in the street, neighbors had called the police and CPS with concerns about the father's violence when he was drinking. However, the child was not placed in foster care at that time because of the lack of evidence regarding child maltreatment. Despite the social support of her sister and help from Emily's grandmother, Mary felt alone and afraid. She was concerned about her daughter and how her well-being would be affected by their home life. She was also stressed by her relationship with her spouse and worried about what would happen when he was released from jail. Although she was trying to make things better, she found it difficult at times to get through the day without feeling sad, afraid, stressed, and overwhelmed with her responsibilities as a mother. Mary had difficulty moving past these feelings to provide Emily with the emotional support she needed.

Application of Framework to Case 1

Emily is 2 years old (24 months), so the treatment choices are ABC, CPP, and PCIT. However, she is presenting with trauma exposure leading to withdrawal behaviors shown especially when she is anxious and her mother is emotionally unavailable. Her wandering in the street and her mother's lack of responsiveness indicate supervisory and emotional neglect, which in addition to the exposure to domestic violence makes PCIT less appropriate. In addition, although separation from the father, who perpetrated domestic violence, may have increased her and her mother's immediate safety, she has experienced the traumatic loss of his responsive caretaking. Emily's traumatic exposure and sequelae point in the direction of either CPP or ABC. The child's behavioral and emotional disturbance is related not only to the traumatic exposure but also to Emily's problematic relationship with her emotionally unavailable and largely unresponsive mother and the absence of her father.

For this case, structured and specific guidance for Emily's mother about ways to override her potentially negative automatic reactions and tune into Emily's changing affect and needs is important. Although both ABC and PCIT offer a more structured approach than CPP, the child is only 24 months old and is not presenting with specific behavior management problems. Therefore, ABC is most appropriate for this case. ABC also offers an excellent opportunity for home-based intervention with this young child and mother. Mary wants to improve Emily's outcomes.

The focus of the work would be to help Mary recognize that her behaviors are neglectful and understand the importance of providing Emily with nurturing and synchronous care. Ultimately, the ABC intervention would guide and support the development of a more positive parent–child relationship to reduce the disorganized attachment behaviors that Emily is demonstrating and help her to develop socioemotional and biological regulatory capacities.

ABC is also indicated because Emily's mother has few resources, presents as depressed, and may have difficulty engaging in clinic-based treatment. In considering retention or duration of access to treatment for Emily and her mother, ABC, which is delivered in the home, is most appropriate. With home-based treatment, Emily's grandmother, who is also a caregiver, can be present, and Emily's mother can learn to engage in nurturing and synchronous parenting behaviors while managing the competing demands of the home environment. For this case, ABC can address many problematic factors in Emily's family and has the highest probability of successful engagement. However, continued monitoring will be important given the potential upheaval when Emily's father returns from jail.

Case 2

Angelina, age 4 years, was referred by CPS because of substantiated reports of physical abuse and child endangerment. Angelina's father, Mr. Kane, reported that she had demonstrated severe tantrums and oppositional behavior since "she's been out of diapers" and indicated that he was "at (his) wit's end with what to do with her." When asked what he had done to address Angelina's behavior in the past, Mr. Kane simply responded, "Everything!" Mr. Kane tearfully confessed that in the midst of one of Angelina's recent tantrums, he struck her across the face and dragged her by the wrist kicking and screaming to the backyard. At that point, he locked Angelina outside to "cool off so I didn't do something I would really regret." Collateral reports from CPS indicated that medical examinations found substantial bruising on Angelina's face and neck in addition to multiple lacerations on her wrist. Neighbors heard Angelina screaming and contacted emergency services. Police reports of the responding officers noted that, on their arrival, Mr. Kane was hostile and told his daughter that the police had finally come to take her away for "being bad."

Mr. Kane denied any prior history of maltreatment or other life-threatening events for either Angelina or himself. He indicated that since his divorce from Angelina's mother, he had begun to struggle financially because of having to balance the responsibilities of working two jobs, caring for Angelina, and paying child support for his other children. Of note, following the divorce, Angelina lived primarily with her mother and two siblings (brother age 9 years and sister age 6 months), only visiting her father every other weekend. However, following Angelina's expulsion from day care for aggressive behaviors toward peers approximately three months previously, Angelina's mother sent her to live with Mr. Kane "until she learned how to act right."

Application of Framework to Case 2

Angelina's age is most appropriate for either PCIT or CPP. If she were younger, ABC would also be an appropriate intervention. The characteristics of trauma exposure, in this case, are interpersonal in nature, and the involved caregiver is the identified perpetrator of the abuse. According to collateral reports, it is possible that Angelina's mother had also engaged in hostile and negative interactions with her daughter; however, at this time there is no protection plan in place for removing Angelina from her father's home. Considering the role of trauma in this case, Angelina's disruptive and aggressive behaviors appear to have long preceded this episode of physical abuse. While doing the evaluation, the clinician has to consider whether this was the first instance when either of Angelina's parents became violent with her. On the basis of the intensity of Angelina's behaviors, however, what is more likely is that the extreme responses represent sequelae of posttraumatic triggering based on prior incidents. Because Mr. Kane's abusive behavior and emotional reactions were extreme, it is likely that he has experienced increasing negative interactions with Angelina and has few child management skills and limited emotional coping capacities, all of which contribute to his dysregulated behaviors and emotions.

The answer to the question "Who is the patient?" is not exactly clear in this case. Angelina's behaviors are severe and had already led to negative outcomes before her placement with her father (i.e., expulsion from preschool and being sent to live with father). At the same time, Mr. Kane is responding to his daughter's behaviors in increasingly dangerous ways. Therefore, the escalating patterns of interaction between Angelina and Mr. Kane appear to be the primary target of treatment. Considering Mr. Kane's denial of prior significant traumas for either himself or his daughter, openness to treatment, and willingness to acknowledge the dangerousness of his behaviors, there do not appear to be parent-centered difficulties that would interfere with his participation in treatment. PCIT has a track record of efficacy in improving severe child behavior problems while reducing future abuse potential in the context of physically abusive caregiver–child relationships. Taking into consideration all these factors, PCIT would likely be the best initial course of treatment for this dyad. It is also important to consider for this case the role of the mother and whether it would be beneficial to the child for the clinician to reach out to her mother to also engage in dyadic treatment. If the mother also agreed to participate in PCIT treatment and the therapist had time, and it was feasible, she or he could conduct two sessions each week, one with each of the parents and Angelina. If that was not logistically possible, then she or he could see the father with the child and the mother with the child every other week.

Case 3

Maurice is a 3½-year-old referred for services by a juvenile court that specializes in handling child welfare cases for young children, age birth to 6 years. Maurice was exposed to extensive sexual abuse by his biological father from age 6 months to 3 years. Maurice's mother had a history of severe alcohol and substance abuse and abandoned him shortly after his birth. All efforts to contact her over the years were unsuccessful. He was removed from his biological parents and placed in the custody of the state (adjudicated dependency) after his father's incarceration for a separate offense. He was placed in foster care where his foster mother reported that he displayed aggressive and developmentally inappropriate sexual behaviors, including self-penetration and simulated sexual intercourse with inanimate objects. He also requested that his foster mother engage in sexual contact with him. Following these reports to the child welfare worker, Maurice was referred to a child advocacy center, where he underwent a forensic interview and medical evaluation. Although Maurice was found to be in good physical health, medical findings were consistent with anal penetration, and Maurice openly disclosed multiple and varied sexual abuse experiences during his interview. He reported that these activities were not only with his biological father but he was also encouraged to engage in sexual activities with his siblings. Other presenting concerns at referral included severe tantrums, developmentally regressed behaviors, dissociative events, attentional problems, hyperactivity, and nightmares. Further, when Maurice's bids for sexual attention and contact with his foster mother were appropriately denied, he would become intensely despondent, withdrawn, or at times, violent. He often asked her, "Why don't you love me?"

Not surprisingly, Maurice's foster mother was overwhelmed by his behavior. Although she was able to understand the connection between his behaviors and prior abuse experiences, she still found his behaviors and requests emotionally disturbing and worried about whether she would be able to deal with them. Despite her initial intentions to adopt, Maurice's foster mother disclosed that she would often find herself withdrawing from Maurice when he was triggered or reacting in intense and/or punitive ways in response to his behavior. In addition, in a courageous moment of self-disclosure, Maurice's foster mother indicated that she also had experienced sexual abuse as a teenager, and seeing Maurice's behavior readily triggered old memories and difficult emotions. She reported often struggling with the reality that he was an innocent child, but, at the same time, she worried that he might also become a perpetrator like the man who abused her.

Application of Framework to Case 3

Maurice's case is complicated. Because of his age, CPP or PCIT is most appropriate. His traumatic exposure is severe, long-standing, and inter-personal in nature. Although his foster mother is not abusive, Maurice experiences her limit setting as rejection. Further, his foster mother is often flooded by unexpected and overwhelming recollections of her abuse experiences when confronted with Maurice's sexual behavior. In making a decision related to treatment in this case, an understanding of the role of trauma in Maurice's behavior is crucial. Although Maurice's actions are extreme and require an effective response, they appear to be best understood as a behavioral reenactment of his prior abuse experiences. This is further supported by his experience of limit setting as interpersonal rejection. Maurice's abuse experiences have led him to develop a working model (internalized understanding about self and others) of loving relationships (between caregiver and child as well as child and child) as sexual in nature. Further, Maurice's other symptoms of nightmares, dissociation, regression, and emotional dysregulation are consistent with presentations of PTSD in young children.

Although PCIT may be effective in reducing his inappropriate behavior (i.e., aggression and tantrums) and increasing positive displays of attention and affection within the dyad, Maurice's posttraumatic symptomatology encompasses far more than the behavioral domain. Considering the primary salience of trauma in addition to severe disruptive behavior, a strong argument can be made for CPP in this case. Further, the role Maurice's foster mother's history plays in their interactions complicates any attempt to answer the question "Who is the patient?" Both Maurice and his foster mother respond to each other's actions, in part, on the basis of prior traumatic experiences and expectations. Although an intervention such as PCIT may be effective at breaking the escalating patterns of negative interactions that are already developing within this dyad, the treatment must focus on many more issues. First, treatment has to directly address Maurice's traumatic experiences, internal representations of relationships, and his caregiver's trauma-based responses to Maurice's behaviors to fully help him process his abuse experiences.

Finally, there do not appear to be contraindications to pursuing CPP treatment with this dyad. Although the foster mother's prior trauma history is clearly important, her level of distress and disorganization do not currently appear to pose a significant risk to the child or for treatment failure. Although PCIT efficacy appears to be lower when caregivers have prior abuse histories, CPP is regularly used with caregivers demonstrating varying levels of posttraumatic stress, with research indicating that CPP leads to reductions in symptoms for both members of the dyad. In assessing family motivation and capacity for longer term treatment, the prognosis, in this case, is positive. Parental rights have been terminated, and the foster parent is motivated and seeking services independently. Considering the primary focus on posttraumatic stress symptomatology (in both the child and caregiver), emphasis should be placed on building healthy attachment and internal representations and reestablishing a normal developmental trajectory and age-appropriate socioemotional responses. CPP appears to be the most appropriate treatment for this case.

Afterword:
Conclusions and
Future Directions

When I (Joy D. Osofsky) started doing research and working with traumatized young children and families over 25 years ago, little was known about infant mental health or the impact of trauma on young children and families. The studies, perspectives, and evidence-based treatment approaches elaborated throughout this volume were either in their infancy or had not yet been conceived of at that time. Only in the past decade has a sound foundation been built on which to base our work in 2016. Many areas have seen significant growth. For example, enormous strides have been made in understanding the brain and the different ways that early experiences affect development.

Two organizations have grown during the past decade in the United States and internationally that have helped to advance the field. The World Association for Infant Mental Health (WAIMH), an organization composed of psychologists, psychiatrists, social workers, and other mental health professionals, was established in 1992. As the first president of WAIMH, I represented a nonmedical professional in a leadership role and

My wonderful colleagues and coauthors, Phillip T. Stepka and Lucy S. King, suggested I write the Afterword for this book providing a perspective on the fields of infant mental health and trauma and directions for the future.

http://dx.doi.org/10.1037/0000030-007
Treating Infants and Young Children Impacted by Trauma: Interventions That Promote Healthy Development, by J. D. Osofsky, P. T. Stepka, and L. S. King

also broadened the emphasis with a strong focus on trauma in the lives of young children.

What is now known as ZERO TO THREE: National Center for Infants, Toddlers and Families (ZTT) began in 1977, with a different name (National Center for Clinical Infant Programs), as a small group of clinicians who came together to share ideas and develop programs that contributed to the emerging field of infant psychiatry. The organization grew large, focusing not just on infant mental health but also on early care and education, parenting, and policy related to young children. During my tenure as president of ZTT, I emphasized the importance of working with infants and toddlers and their families exposed to trauma and developed with ZTT the Safe Babies Court Teams (SBCT). The SBCTs provide specialized multidisciplinary programming in juvenile courts and transform the role of child welfare using the science of early child development to emphasize child well-being. The SBCTs have resulted in young children who have been adjudicated dependent by the courts because of abuse and neglect achieving permanency more quickly either with a biological parent or relative or through adoption. Young children who are seen in these specialized courts are also significantly less likely to be exposed to maltreatment in the future. Both WAIMH and ZTT, two organizations with very different structures, have contributed a developmental and clinical understanding of infancy and early development.

In addition, over a decade ago, the Irving Harris Foundation established the Professional Development Network to develop and expand infant mental health training. This network consists of 18 early childhood and infant mental health leadership sites located in 10 states, the District of Columbia, and Israel. We are fortunate at the Louisiana State University Health Sciences Center (LSUHSC) to have the LSUHSC Harris Center for Infant Mental Health, which in collaboration with the other Harris programs has driven the development and expansion of infant mental health training.

The main goal of this volume has been to describe the impact of trauma on young children and elucidate the ways in which children and families can be helped through evidence-based treatments. Through the Violence Intervention Program developed in the 1990s, in partnership with the New Orleans Police Department, we learned that young children frequently witnessed violence in their neighborhoods, with parents and other adults being unaware of the negative effects this has on their homes or neighborhoods. Many people believed children were too young to be affected or that they would "get over it." Even professionals were much less aware than they are today of the immediate and long-term impact of witnessing violence. As we described in the Introduction, the negative effects of adverse childhood experiences on development and health are finally being widely recognized and addressed, largely thanks to studies done in the past 2 decades. Together we worked to help families learn how to protect their children from violence exposure and to help find positive, nurturing, and safe activities for children living in urban neighborhoods with much violence. At about the same time, we developed programs for adolescent mothers in collaboration with community groups. In these intervention programs, we learned new ways to communicate with the young mothers and developed an intervention, "Speaking for Baby" (Carter, Osofsky, & Hann, 1991), that improved outcomes in mothers and increased maternal sensitivity.

The LSUHSC team has learned a great deal about trauma prevention, response, and recovery in young children through our work with the National Child Traumatic Stress Network (NCTSN). Our NCTSN centers have been involved collaboratively with others in helping to develop more trauma-informed child-serving systems of care, such as schools, child welfare, law enforcement, and juvenile court, and in disseminating evidence-based treatments for young children. In the past decade, significant advances have been made in understanding the impact of trauma on the developing brain. The Center for the Developing Child at Harvard, initiated in 2006, has taken the science of early psychobiological development and translated it to be more accessible to a multidisciplinary group. Through creative translational work, this group and others have expanded the reach and understanding of complex biological mechanisms that confer risk of long-term problems in children exposed to early trauma.

In infant mental health, much is also now known about ways to systematically use observations for both assessment and treatment to gain more understanding of young children and their relationships long before they are able to describe their thoughts and feelings using language. For psychologists and other mental health professionals, when young children present with problems, too often the focus is on the symptoms and what is going wrong with the child. Not enough emphasis is placed on possibilities and pathways for recovery or on the importance of resilience and mental wellness.

This volume provides information and perspectives that can influence the way clinicians understand and work with infants, young children, and families who have been exposed to trauma. It is crucial that this material is integrated into mental health training programs to increase knowledge of infant and young child mental health and stress the importance of evaluation, assessment, and evidence-based treatments for these young children. Although this knowledge is specialized, it is broadly applicable. Clinicians who work solely with adults will encounter issues of infant and young child mental health when their clients, now parents, present with problems of stress and coping involving their own children. Others who work with older children and adolescents may contend with the lasting effects of trauma experienced in the first years of life. Integration of knowledge related to the impact of trauma on infant and young child mental health into training programs will facilitate the capacity of future clinicians to provide services for patients across the lifespan.

From a public policy perspective, important and impactful progress has been made in raising awareness of mental health issues. However, the majority of efforts have focused on older youth and adults. Encouragingly, legislation and public policy are increasingly emphasizing the needs of very young children. This book details research and clinical work indicating that for far too many young children, problems begin during the first years of life, which set children on pathways riddled with developmental, behavioral, emotional, and mental health challenges. Directions for the future must include a public health and educational investment in prevention, intervention, and treatment for young children exposed to trauma, including wide dissemination of evidence-based programs. To expand both knowledge about and availability of services for young children and families, much more education is needed not only for mental health providers but also for the public, along with increased outreach efforts and professional training related to the impact of trauma on young children. Over time, such public policy efforts will help to improve the public health response to violence exposure. It is important to address disparities in care and increase the continuity of care for young children affected by trauma through timely identification, intervention, and treatment.

Young children are a vulnerable and underserved group. It is crucial to recognize that prevention is an important part of the work we do in increasing care and improving outcomes for this group. The first years of life are a sensitive period in which developmental systems are rapidly changing; therefore, intervention must occur early. Although negative experiences during this period are more likely to be detrimental to well-being, positive experiences may also have particularly powerful effects. In particular, the earlier safety is ensured and caregiving is improved, the better the outcomes for young children and their families. We are hopeful that the theoretical, research-based, and clinical information presented in this book will aid our readers in advancing work related to the impact and treatment of trauma exposure in young children. Furthermore, we hope that this information clarifies why we should not "wait" with young children. Rather, the biological, cognitive, and socioemotional conse-quences of trauma must be recognized and addressed early.

Appendix:
Key Points on the Impact of Early Trauma on Development

BIOLOGICAL DEVELOPMENT

- Trauma has a negative impact on the biological systems that control how children react to and regulate emotions and stress; however, positive caregiving appears to facilitate adaptive reactivity and regulation.
- Trauma appears to alter the development of brain structures. Researchers have identified changes in the volumes of multiple cortical and subcortical structures.
- Trauma may change how genes are expressed, which is a potential cause of early problems in functioning among trauma-exposed children.

COGNITIVE AND LINGUISTIC DEVELOPMENT

- The direct actions of caregivers (e.g., support), as well as familial risk factors (e.g., poverty), affect cognitive and linguistic development.
- Children exposed to neglect or violence demonstrate deficits in executive function, language, IQ, and academic achievement.
- Improved caregiving fosters recovery of cognitive and linguistic function.

SOCIOEMOTIONAL DEVELOPMENT

- Problems in emotion regulation emerge both when children are exposed to maltreatment and when they have caregivers who are traumatized.
- Young children rely on caregivers to assist in their emotion regulation. They mirror the regulation patterns of caregivers such that impaired caregiver emotion regulation can compromise their own.
- Exposure to trauma in early life may compromise attachment relationships.

References

Aber, J. L., & Cicchetti, D. (1984). The socio-emotional development of mal-treated children: An empirical and theoretical analysis. In H. Fitzgerald, B. Lester, & M. Yogman (Eds.), *Theory and research in behavioral pediatrics* (Vol. 2, pp. 147–205). New York, NY: Plenum Press. http://dx.doi.org/10.1007/978-1-4899-1660-0_5

Achenbach, T. M., & Rescorla, L. A. (2001). *Manual for the ASEBA School-Age Forms & Profiles.* Burlington: University of Vermont, Research Center for Children, Youth, & Families.

Adoption and Safe Families Act of 1997, Pub. L. No. 105-89 (1997).

Ainsworth, M. D. S. (1989). Attachments beyond infancy. *American Psychologist, 44,* 709–716. http://dx.doi.org/10.1037/0003-066X.44.4.709

Ainsworth, M. D. S., Blehar, M. C., Waters, E., & Wall, S. (1978). *Patterns of attachment: A psychological study of the strange situation.* Hillsdale, NJ: Erlbaum.

Appleyard, K., Berlin, L. J., Rosanbalm, K. D., & Dodge, K. A. (2011). Preventing early child maltreatment: Implications from a longitudinal study of maternal abuse history, substance use problems, and offspring victimization. *Prevention Science, 12,* 139–149. http://dx.doi.org/10.1007/s11121-010-0193-2

Bagner, D. M., & Eyberg, S. M. (2007). Parent–child interaction therapy for disruptive behavior in children with mental retardation: A randomized controlled trial. *Journal of Clinical Child and Adolescent Psychology, 36,* 418–429. http://dx.doi.org/10.1080/15374410701448448

Bakermans-Kranenburg, M. J., van IJzendoorn, M. H., & Juffer, F. (2005). Disorganized infant attachment and preventive interventions: A review and meta-analysis. *Infant Mental Health Journal, 26,* 191–216. http://dx.doi.org/10.1002/imhj.20046

Baldwin, D. A., & Moses, L. J. (1996). The ontogeny of social information gathering. *Child Development, 67,* 1915–1939. http://dx.doi.org/10.2307/1131601

Baumrind, D. (1966). Effects of authoritative parental control on child behavior. *Child Development, 37,* 887–907. http://dx.doi.org/10.2307/1126611

Baumrind, D. (1967). Child care practices anteceding three patterns of preschool behavior. *Genetic Psychology Monographs, 75,* 43–88.

Berliner, L., & Elliott, D. M. (2002). Sexual abuse of children. In J. E. B. Myers, L. Berliner, J. Briere, C. T. Hendrix, C. Jenny, & T. Reid (Eds.), *The APSAC handbook on child maltreatment* (2nd ed., pp. 55–78). Thousand Oaks, CA: Sage.

Bernard, K., Dozier, M., Bick, J., & Gordon, M. K. (2015). Intervening to enhance cortisol regulation among children at risk for neglect: Results of a randomized clinical trial. *Development and Psychopathology, 27,* 829–841. http://dx.doi.org/10.1017/S095457941400073X

Bernard, K., Dozier, M., Bick, J., Lewis-Morrarty, E., Lindhiem, O., & Carlson, E. (2012). Enhancing attachment organization among maltreated children: Results of a randomized clinical trial. *Child Development, 83,* 623–636.

Bernard, K., Hostinar, C. E., & Dozier, M. (2015, February). Intervention effects on diurnal cortisol rhythms of Child Protective Services-referred infants in early childhood. *JAMA Pediatrics, 169,* 112–119. http://dx.doi.org/10.1001/jamapediatrics.2014.2369

Bernard, K., Meade, E. B., & Dozier, M. (2013). Parental synchrony and nurturance as targets in an attachment based intervention: Building upon Mary Ainsworth's insights about mother–infant interaction. *Attachment & Human Development, 15,* 507–523. http://dx.doi.org/10.1080/14616734.2013.820920

Bernard, K., Simons, R., & Dozier, M. (2015). Effects of an attachment-based intervention on Child Protective Services-referred mothers' event-related potentials to children's emotions. *Child Development, 86,* 1673–1684. http://dx.doi.org/10.1111/cdev.12418

Bernard, K., Zwerling, J., & Dozier, M. (2015). Effects of early adversity on young children's diurnal cortisol rhythms and externalizing behavior. *Developmental Psychobiology, 57,* 935–947. http://dx.doi.org/10.1002/dev.21324

Bick, J., & Dozier, M. (2013). The effectiveness of an attachment-based intervention in promoting foster mothers' sensitivity toward foster infants. *Infant Mental Health Journal, 34,* 95–103. http://dx.doi.org/10.1002/imhj.21373

Bock, J., Wainstock, T., Braun, K., & Segal, M. (2015). Stress in utero: Prenatal programming of brain plasticity and cognition. *Biological Psychiatry, 78,* 315–326. http://dx.doi.org/10.1016/j.biopsych.2015.02.036

Boggs, S., Eyberg, S., & Reynolds, L. A. (1990). Concurrent validity of the Eyberg Child Behavior Inventory. *Journal of Clinical Child Psychology, 19,* 75–78. http://dx.doi.org/10.1207/s15374424jccp1901_9

Boggs, S. R., Eyberg, S. M., Edwards, D. L., Rayfield, A., Jacobs, J., Bagner, D., & Hood, K. K. (2005). Outcomes of parent–child interaction therapy: A comparison of treatment completers and study dropouts one to three years later. *Child & Family Behavior Therapy, 26*, 1–22. http://dx.doi.org/10.1300/J019v26n04_01

Bonanno, G. A., Westphal, M., & Mancini, A. D. (2011). Resilience to loss and potential trauma. *Annual Review of Clinical Psychology, 7*, 511–35. http://dx.doi.org/10.1146/annurev-clinpsy-032210-104526

Borrego, J., Jr., Gutow, M. R., Reicher, S., & Barker, C. (2008). Parent–child interaction therapy with domestic violence populations. *Journal of Family Violence, 23*, 495–505. http://dx.doi.org/10.1007/s10896-008-9177-4

Bosquet Enlow, M., Blood, E., & Egeland, B. (2013). Sociodemographic risk, developmental competence, and PTSD symptoms in young children exposed to interpersonal trauma in early life. *Journal of Traumatic Stress, 26*, 686–694. http://dx.doi.org/10.1002/jts.21866

Bosquet Enlow, M., Egeland, B., Blood, E. A., Wright, R. O., & Wright, R. J. (2012). Interpersonal trauma exposure and cognitive development in children to age 8 years: A longitudinal study. *Journal of Epidemiology and Community Health, 66*, 1005–1010. http://dx.doi.org/10.1136/jech-2011-200727

Bosquet Enlow, M., Egeland, B., Carlson, E., Blood, E., & Wright, R. J. (2014). Mother–infant attachment and the intergenerational transmission of post-traumatic stress disorder. *Development and Psychopathology, 26*, 41–65. http://dx.doi.org/10.1017/S0954579413000515

Bosquet Enlow, M., King, L., Schreier, H. M., Howard, J. M., Rosenfield, D., Ritz, T., & Wright, R. J. (2014). Maternal sensitivity and infant autonomic and endocrine stress responses. *Early Human Development, 90*, 377–385. http://dx.doi.org/10.1016/j.earlhumdev.2014.04.007

Bowlby, J. (1988). *A secure base: Parent–child attachments and healthy human development.* New York, NY: Basic Books.

Brestan, E. V., Eyberg, S. M., Boggs, S. R., & Algina, J. (1997). Parent–child interaction therapy: Parents' perceptions of untreated siblings. *Child & Family Behavior Therapy, 19*, 13–28. http://dx.doi.org/10.1300/J019v19n03_02

Bretherton, I., Oppenheim, D., Buchsbaum, H., Emde, R. N., & the MacArthur Narrative Group. (1990). *The MacArthur Story Stem Battery (MSSB).* Unpublished manuscript, University of Wisconsin-Madison.

Briggs-Gowan, M. J., Carter, A. S., & Ford, J. D. (2012). Parsing the effects violence exposure in early childhood: Modeling developmental pathways. *Journal of Pediatric Psychology, 37*, 11–22. http://dx.doi.org/10.1093/jpepsy/jsr063

Briggs-Gowan, M. J., Ford, J. D., Fraleigh, L., McCarthy, K., & Carter, A. S. (2010). Prevalence of exposure to potentially traumatic events in a healthy birth cohort of very young children in the northeastern United States. *Journal of Traumatic Stress, 23,* 725–733.

Bruce, J., Fisher, P. A., Pears, K. C., & Levine, S. (2009). Morning cortisol levels in preschool-aged foster children: Differential effects of maltreatment type. *Developmental Psychobiology, 51,* 14–23. http://dx.doi.org/10.1002/dev.20333

California Evidence-Based Clearinghouse for Child Welfare. (2016). *Welcome to the CEBC: The California Evidence-Based Clearinghouse for Child Welfare.* Retrieved from http://www.cebc4cw.org/

Calkins, S. D., & Hill, A. (2007). Caregiver influences on emerging emotion regulation: Biological and environmental transactions in early development. In J. J. Gross (Ed.), *Handbook of emotion regulation* (pp. 229–248). New York, NY: Guilford Press.

Callaghan, B. L., & Tottenham, N. (2016). The neuro-environmental loop of plasticity: A cross-species analysis of parental effects on emotion circuitry development following typical and adverse caregiving. *Neuropsychopharmacology, 41,* 163–176. http://dx.doi.org/10.1038/npp.2015.204

Carlson, E. A. (1998). A prospective longitudinal study of attachment disorganization/disorientation. *Child Development, 69,* 1107–1128. http://dx.doi.org/10.1111/j.1467-8624.1998.tb06163.x

Caron, E. B., Bernard, K., & Dozier, M. (2016). In vivo feedback predicts behavioral change in the attachment and biobehavioral catch-up intervention. *Journal of Clinical Child and Adolescent Psychology.* Advance online publication. http://dx.doi.org/10.1080/15374416.2016.1141359

Caron, E. B., Weston-Lee, P., Haggerty, D., & Dozier, M. (2015). Community implementation outcomes of attachment and biobehavioral catch-up. *Child Abuse and Neglect, 53,* 128–137. http://dx.doi.org/10.1016/j.chiabu.2015.11.010

Carter, S., Osofsky, J. D., & Hann, D. M. (1991). Speaking for baby: Therapeutic interventions with adolescent mothers and their infants. *Infant Mental Health Journal, 12,* 291–301. http://dx.doi.org/10.1002/1097-0355(199124)12:4<291::AID-IMHJ2280120403>3.0.CO;2-3

Chadwick Center on Children and Families. (2004). *Closing the quality chasm in child abuse treatment: Identifying and disseminating best practices.* San Diego, CA: Author.

Chaffin, M., Funderburk, B., Bard, D., Valle, L. A., & Gurwitch, R. (2011). A combined motivation and parent–child interaction therapy package reduces child welfare recidivism in a randomized dismantling field trial. *Journal of Consulting and Clinical Psychology, 79,* 84–95. http://dx.doi.org/10.1037/a0021227

Chaffin, M., Silovsky, J. F., Funderburk, B., Valle, L. A., Brestan, E. V., Balachova, T., . . . Bonner, B. L. (2004). Parent–child interaction therapy with physically abusive parents: Efficacy for reducing future abuse reports. *Journal of Consulting and Clinical Psychology, 72*, 500–510. http://dx.doi.org/ 10.1037/0022-006X.72.3.500

Chaffin, M., Valle, L. A., Funderburk, B., Gurwitch, R., Silovsky, J., Bard, D., . . . Kees, M. (2009). A motivational intervention can improve retention in PCIT for low-motivation child welfare clients. *Child Maltreatment, 14*, 356–368. http://dx.doi.org/10.1177/1077559509332263

Chase, R. M., & Eyberg, S. M. (2008). Clinical presentation and treatment outcome for children with comorbid externalizing and internalizing symptoms. *Journal of Anxiety Disorders, 22*, 273–282. http://dx.doi.org/10.1016/ j.janxdis.2007.03.006

Chen, C. (2014). *A hidden crisis: Findings on adverse childhood experiences in California.* Retrieved from Center for Youth Wellness website: http://www. centerforyouthwellness.org/blog/BFRSS

Chen, M. C., Hamilton, J. P., & Gotlib, I. H. (2010). Decreased hippocampal volume in healthy girls at risk of depression. *Archives of General Psychiatry, 67*, 270–276. http://dx.doi.org/10.1001/archgenpsychiatry.2009.202

Child Welfare Information Gateway. (2015). *Child abuse and neglect fatalities 2013: Statistics and interventions.* Washington, DC: U.S. Department of Health and Human Services, Children's Bureau.

Cicchetti, D., & Rogosch, F. A. (2001). The impact of child maltreatment and psychopathology on neuroendocrine functioning. *Development and Psychopathology, 13*, 783–804.

Cicchetti, D., Rogosch, F. A., & Toth, S. L. (2006). Fostering secure attachment in infants in maltreating families through preventive interventions. *Development and Psychopathology, 18*, 623–649. http://dx.doi.org/10.1017/ S0954579406060329

Cicchetti, D., Rogosch, F. A., Toth, S. L., & Sturge-Apple, M. L. (2011). Normalizing the development of cortisol regulation in maltreated infants through preventive interventions. *Development and Psychopathology, 23*, 789–800. http:// dx.doi.org/10.1017/S0954579411000307

Cicchetti, D., & Valentino, K. (2006). An ecological–transactional perspective on child maltreatment: Failure of the average expectable environment and its influence on child development. In D. Cicchetti & D. J. Cohen (Eds.), *Developmental psychopathology* (2nd ed., Vol. 3, pp. 129–201). Hoboken, NJ: Wiley.

Conradt, E., Lester, B. M., Appleton, A. A., Armstrong, D. A., & Marsit, C. J. (2013). The roles of DNA methylation of NR3C1 and 11b-HSD2 and exposure to maternal mood disorder in utero on newborn neurobehavior. *Epigenetics, 8*, 1321–1329. http://dx.doi.org/10.4161/epi.26634

Courtois, C. A., & Gold, S. N. (2009). The need for inclusion of psychological trauma in the professional curriculum: A call to action. *Psychological Trauma: Theory, Research, Practice, and Policy, 1,* 3–23.

Cowell, R. A., Cicchetti, D., Rogosch, F. A., & Toth, S. L. (2015). Childhood maltreatment and its effect on neurocognitive functioning: Timing and chronicity matter. *Development and Psychopathology, 27,* 521–533. http://dx.doi.org/10.1017/S0954579415000139

Curtiss, S. (1977). *Genie: A psycholinguistic study of a modern-day "wild child."* New York, NY: Academic Press.

Cyr, C., Euser, E. M., Bakermans-Kranenburg, M. J., & van IJzendoorn, M. H. (2010). Attachment security and disorganization in maltreating and high-risk families: A series of meta-analyses. *Development and Psychopathology, 22,* 87–108. http://dx.doi.org/10.1017/S0954579409990289

Dannlowski, U., Stuhrmann, A., Beutelmann, V., Zwanzger, P., Lenzen, T., Grotegerd, D., . . . Kugel, H. (2012). Limbic scars: Long-term consequences of childhood maltreatment revealed by functional and structural magnetic resonance imaging. *Biological Psychiatry, 71,* 286–293. http://dx.doi.org/10.1016/j.biopsych.2011.10.021

De Bellis, M. D., Hooper, S. R., Spratt, E. G., & Woolley, D. P. (2009). Neuropsychological findings in childhood neglect and their relationships to pediatric PTSD. *Journal of the International Neuropsychological Society, 15,* 868–878. http://dx.doi.org/10.1017/S1355617709990464

DePrince, A. P., & Newman, E. (2011). The art and science of trauma-focused training and education. *Psychological Trauma: Theory, Research, Practice, and Policy, 3,* 13–14.

Dierckx, B., Dieleman, G., Tulen, J. H. M., Treffers, P. D. A., Utens, E. M. W. J., Verhulst, F. C., & Tiemeier, H. (2012). Persistence of anxiety disorders and concomitant changes in cortisol. *Journal of Anxiety Disorders, 26,* 635–641. http://dx.doi.org/10.1016/j.janxdis.2012.04.001

Doom, J. R., Cicchetti, D., & Rogosch, F. A. (2014). Longitudinal patterns of cortisol regulation differ in maltreated and nonmaltreated children. *Journal of the American Academy of Child and Adolescent Psychiatry, 53,* 1206–1215. http://dx.doi.org/10.1016/j.jaac.2014.08.006

Dozier, M., Bick, J., & Bernard, K. (2011). Attachment-based treatment for young, vulnerable children. In J. D. Osofsky (Ed.), *Clinical work with traumatized young children* (pp. 295–312). New York, NY: Guilford Press.

Dozier, M., Lindhiem, O., Lewis, E., Bick, J., Bernard, K., & Peloso, E. (2009). Effects of a foster parent training program on young children's attachment behaviors: Preliminary evidence from a randomized clinical trial. *Child*

& Adolescent Social Work Journal, 26, 321–332. http://dx.doi.org/10.1007/s10560-009-0165-1

Dozier, M., Meade, E., & Bernard, K. (2014). Attachment and biobehavioral catch-up: an intervention for parents at risk of maltreating their infants and toddlers. In S. Timmer & A. Urquiza (Eds.), *Evidence-based approaches for the treatment of maltreated children* (pp. 43–59). Dordrecht, Netherlands: Springer. http://dx.doi.org/10.1007/978-94-007-7404-9_4

Dozier, M., Peloso, E., Lindhiem, O., Gordon, M. K., Manni, M., Sepulveda, S., . . . Levine, S. (2006). Developing evidence-based interventions for foster children: An example of a randomized clinical trial with infants and toddlers. *Journal of Social Issues, 62*, 767–785. http://dx.doi.org/10.1111/j.1540-4560.2006.00486.x

Dozier, M., Stoval, K. C., Albus, K. E., & Bates, B. (2001). Attachment for infants in foster care: The role of caregiver state of mind. *Child Development, 72*, 1467–1477. http://dx.doi.org/10.1111/1467-8624.00360

Egger, H. L., & Emde, R. N. (2011). Developmentally sensitive diagnostic criteria for mental health disorders in early childhood: The *Diagnostic and Statistical Manual of Mental Disorders—IV*, the Research Diagnostic Criteria–Preschool Age, and the Diagnostic Classification of Mental Health and Developmental Disorders of Infancy and Early Childhood–Revised. *American Psychologist, 66*, 95–106. http://dx.doi.org/10.1037/a0021026

Eigsti, I. M., & Cicchetti, D. (2004). The impact of child maltreatment on expressive syntax at 60 months. *Developmental Science, 7*, 88–102. http://dx.doi.org/10.1111/j.1467-7687.2004.00325.x

Ellis, B. J., Boyce, W. T., Belsky, J., Bakermans-Kranenburg, M. J., & van IJzendoorn, M. H. (2011). Differential susceptibility to the environment: An evolutionary-neurodevelopmental theory. *Development and Psychopathology, 23*, 7–28. http://dx.doi.org/10.1017/S0954579410000611

Entringer, S., Epel, E. S., Kumsta, R., Lin, J., Hellhammer, D. H., Blackburn, E. H., . . . Wadhwa, P. D. (2011). Stress exposure in intrauterine life is associated with shorter telomere length in young adulthood. *Proceedings of the National Academy of Sciences of the United States of America, 108*, E513–E518. http://dx.doi.org/10.1073/pnas.1107759108

Essex, M. J., Boyce, W. T., Hertzman, C., Lam, L. L., Armstrong, J. M., Neumann, S. M., & Kobor, M. S. (2013). Epigenetic vestiges of early developmental adversity: Childhood stress exposure and DNA methylation in adolescence. *Child Development, 84*, 58–75. http://dx.doi.org/10.1111/j.1467-8624.2011.01641.x

Evans, G. W. (2004). The environment of childhood poverty. *American Psychologist, 59*, 77–92. http://dx.doi.org/10.1037/0003-066X.59.2.77

Eyberg, S. (1988). Parent–child interaction therapy: Integration of traditional and behavioral concerns. *Child & Family Behavior Therapy, 10*, 33–46. http://dx.doi.org/10.1300/J019v10n01_04

Eyberg, S. M., Chase, R. M., Fernandez, M. A., & Nelson, M. M. (2014). *Dyadic parent–child interaction coding system (DPICS) clinical manual* (4th ed.). Gainesville, FL: PCIT International.

Eyberg, S. M., & Pincus, D. (1999). *Eyberg Child Behavior Inventory and Sutter-Eyberg Student Behavior Inventory–Revised.* Odessa, FL: Psychological Assessment Resources.

Eyberg, S. M., & Ross, A. W. (1978). Assessment of child behavior problems: The validation of a new inventory. *Journal of Clinical Child Psychology, 7*, 113–116. http://dx.doi.org/10.1080/15374417809532835

Feldman, R., Singer, M., & Zagoory, O. (2010). Touch attenuates infants' physiological reactivity to stress. *Developmental Science, 13*, 271–278. http://dx.doi.org/10.1111/j.1467-7687.2009.00890.x

Felitti, V. J., & Anda, R. F. (2010). The relationship of adverse childhood experiences to adult medical disease, psychiatric disorders and sexual behavior: Implications for healthcare. In R. A. Lanius, E. Vermetten, & C. Pain (Eds.), *The impact of early life trauma on health and disease: The hidden epidemic* (pp. 77–87). New York, NY: Cambridge University Press. http://dx.doi.org/10.1017/CBO9780511777042.010

Felitti, V. J., Anda, R. F., Nordenberg, D., Williamson, D. F., Spitz, A. M., Edwards, V., . . . Marks, J. S. (1998). Relationship of childhood abuse and household dysfunction to many of the leading causes of death in adults: The Adverse Childhood Experiences (ACE) Study. *American Journal of Preventive Medicine, 14*, 245–258. http://dx.doi.org/10.1016/S0749-3797(98)00017-8

Fernald, A., Marchman, V. A., & Weisleder, A. (2013). SES differences in language processing skill and vocabulary are evident at 18 months. *Developmental Science, 16*, 234–248. http://dx.doi.org/10.1111/desc.12019

Fernandez, M. A., Butler, A. M., & Eyberg, S. M. (2011). Treatment outcome for low socioeconomic status African American families in parent–child interaction therapy: A pilot study. *Child & Family Behavior Therapy, 33*, 32–48. http://dx.doi.org/10.1080/07317107.2011.545011

Finkelhor, D., Ormrod, R. K., & Turner, H. A. (2007). Poly-victimization: A neglected component in child victimization. *Child Abuse & Neglect, 31*, 7–26. http://dx.doi.org/10.1016/j.chiabu.2006.06.008

Finkelhor, D., Turner, H., Hamby, S. L., & Ormrod, R. (2011). Polyvictimization: Children's exposure to multiple types of violence, crime, and abuse. *Juvenile Justice Bulletin.* Retrieved from https://www.ncjrs.gov/pdffiles1/ojjdp/235504.pdf

Fonagy, P., Cottrell, D., Phillips, J., Bevington, D., Glaser, D., & Allison, E. (2014). *What works for whom? A critical review of treatments for children and adolescents.* New York, NY: Guilford Press.

Fraiberg, S., Adelson, E., & Shapiro, V. (1975). Ghosts in the nursery: A psychoanalytic approach to the problems of impaired infant–mother relationships. *Journal of the American Academy of Child Psychiatry, 14,* 387–421. http://dx.doi.org/10.1016/S0002-7138(09)61442-4

Franks, B. A. (2011). Moving targets: A developmental framework for understanding children's changes following disasters. *Journal of Applied Developmental Psychology, 32,* 58–69. http://dx.doi.org/10.1016/j.appdev.2010.12.004

Fredrickson, B. L. (2004). The broaden-and-build theory of positive emotions. *Philosophical Transactions of the Royal Society of London: Series B. Biological Sciences, 359,* 1367–1378. http://dx.doi.org/10.1098/rstb.2004.1512

Funderburk, B. W., & Eyberg, S. M. (1989). Psychometric characteristics of the Sutter-Eyberg Student Behavior Inventory: A school behavior rating scale for use with preschool children. *Behavioral Assessment, 11,* 297–313.

Gee, D. G., Gabard-Durnam, L., Telzer, E. H., Humphreys, K. L., Goff, B., Shapiro, M., . . . Tottenham, N. (2014). Maternal buffering of human amygdala-prefrontal circuitry during childhood but not during adolescence. *Psychological Science, 25,* 2067–2078. http://dx.doi.org/10.1177/0956797614550878

Gee, D. G., Gabard-Durnam, L. J., Flannery, J., Goff, B., Humphreys, K. L., Telzer, E. H., . . . Tottenham, N. (2013a). Early developmental emergence of human amygdala-prefrontal connectivity after maternal deprivation. *Proceedings of the National Academy of Sciences of the United States of America, 110,* 15638–15643. http://dx.doi.org/10.1073/pnas.1307893110

Gee, D. G., Humphreys, K. L., Flannery, J., Goff, B., Telzer, E. H., Shapiro, M., . . . Tottenham, N. (2013b). A developmental shift from positive to negative connectivity in human amygdala–prefrontal circuitry. *Journal of Neuroscience, 33,* 4584–4593.

Ghosh Ippen, C., Ford, J., Racusin, R., Acker, M., Bosquet, M., Rogers, K., . . . Edwards, J. (2002). *Traumatic Events Screening Inventory–Parent Report Revised.* Dartmouth, NH: National Center for PTSD Dartmouth Child Trauma Research Group.

Ghosh Ippen, C., & Lewis, M. L. (2011). "They just don't get it": A diversity-informed approach to understanding engagement. In J. D. Osofsky (Ed.), *Clinical work with traumatized young children* (pp. 31–52). New York, NY: Guilford Press.

Graham, A. M., Fisher, P. A., & Pfeifer, J. H. (2013). What sleeping babies hear: A functional MRI study of interparental conflict and infants' emotion processing. *Psychological Science Current Issue, 24,* 782–789. http://dx.doi.org/10.1177/0956797612458803

Green, J. G., McLaughlin, K. A., Berglund, P. A., Gruber, M. J., Sampson, N. A., Zaslavsky, A. M., & Kessler, R. C. (2010). Childhood adversities and adult psychiatric disorders in the national comorbidity survey replication I: Associations with first onset of *DSM–IV* disorders. *Archives of General Psychiatry, 67*, 113–123. http://dx.doi.org/10.1001/archgenpsychiatry.2009.186

Gross, J. J. (2013). Emotion regulation: Taking stock and moving forward. *Emotion, 13*, 359–365. http://dx.doi.org/10.1037/a0032135

Groves, B. M., Zuckerman, B., Marans, S., & Cohen, D. J. (1993, January 13). Silent victims: Children who witness violence. *JAMA, 269*, 262–264. http://dx.doi.org/10.1001/jama.1993.03500020096039

Gunnar, M., & Quevedo, K. (2007). The neurobiology of stress and development. *Annual Review of Psychology, 58*, 145–173. http://dx.doi.org/10.1146/annurev.psych.58.110405.085605

Hakman, M., Chaffin, M., Funderburk, B., & Silovsky, J. F. (2009). Change trajectories for parent–child interaction sequences during parent–child interaction therapy for child physical abuse. *Child Abuse & Neglect, 33*, 461–470. http://dx.doi.org/10.1016/j.chiabu.2008.08.003

Halle, T., Forry, N., Hair, E., Perper, K., Wandner, L., Wessel, J., & Vick, J. (2009). *Disparities in early learning and development: Lessons from the Early Childhood Longitudinal Study–Birth Cohort (ECLS-B)*. Washington, DC: Child Trends.

Hamby, S., Finkelhor, D., Turner, H., & Ormrod, R. (2011). Children's exposure to intimate partner violence and other family violence. *Juvenile Justice Bulletin*. Retrieved from https://www.ncjrs.gov/pdffiles1/ojjdp/232272.pdf

Hancock, K. J., Mitrou, F., Shipley, M., Lawrence, D., & Zubrick, S. R. (2013). A three generation study of the mental health relationships between grandparents, parents and children. *BMC Psychiatry, 13*, 299. http://dx.doi.org/10.1186/1471-244X-13-299

Hanf, C. (1969, June). *A two-stage program for modifying maternal controlling during mother–child (M–C) interaction*. Paper presented at the Western Psychological Association Meeting, Vancouver, Canada.

Hart, B. B., & Risley, T. R. (2003). The early catastrophe: The 30 million word gap. *American Educator, 27*, 4–9.

Hayes, L. J., Goodman, S. H., & Carlson, E. (2013). Maternal antenatal depression and infant disorganized attachment at 12 months. *Attachment & Human Development, 15*, 133–153. http://dx.doi.org/10.1080/14616734.2013.743256

Health Federation of Philadelphia. (2016). *The Philadelphia Urban ACE Study*. Retrieved from http://www.instituteforsafefamilies.org/philadelphia-urban-ace-study

Hesse, E., & Main, M. (1999). Second-generation effects of unresolved trauma in nonmaltreating parents: Dissociated, frightened, and threatening parental behavior. *Psychoanalytic Inquiry, 19*, 481–540. http://dx.doi.org/10.1080/07351699909534265

Hodel, A. S., Hunt, R. H., Cowell, R. A., Van Den Heuvel, S. E., Gunnar, M. R., & Thomas, K. M. (2015). Duration of early adversity and structural brain development in post-institutionalized adolescents. *NeuroImage, 105*, 112–119. http://dx.doi.org/10.1016/j.neuroimage.2014.10.020

Hood, K. K., & Eyberg, S. M. (2003). Outcomes of parent–child interaction therapy: Mothers' reports of maintenance three to six years after treatment. *Journal of Clinical Child and Adolescent Psychology, 32*, 419–429. http://dx.doi.org/10.1207/S15374424JCCP3203_10

Howard, M. L., & Tener, R. R. (2008). Children who have been traumatized: One court's response. *Juvenile & Family Court Journal, 59*, 21–34. http://dx.doi.org/10.1111/j.1755-6988.2008.00019.x

Hughes, C. H., & Ensor, R. A. (2009). How do families help or hinder the emergence of early executive function? *New Directions in Child and Adolescent Development, 123*, 35–50.

Humphreys, K. L., & Zeanah, C. H. (2015). Deviations from the expectable environment in early childhood and emerging psychopathology. *Neuropsychopharmacology, 40*, 154–170. http://dx.doi.org/10.1038/npp.2014.165

Isaksson, J., Nilsson, K. W., Nyberg, F., Hogmark, A., & Lindblad, F. (2012). Cortisol levels in children with attention-deficit/hyperactivity disorder. *Journal of Psychiatric Research, 46*, 1398–1405. http://dx.doi.org/10.1016/j.jpsychires.2012.08.021

Jaffee, S. R., Bowes, L., Ouellet-Morin, I., Fisher, H. L., Moffitt, T. E., Merrick, M. T., & Aresenault, L. (2013). Safe, stable, nurturing relationships break the intergenerational cycle of abuse: A prospective nationally representative cohort of children in the United Kingdom. *Journal of Adolescent Health, 53*, S4–S10. http://dx.doi.org/10.1016/j.jadohealth.2013.04.007

Jaffee, S. R., McFarquhar, T., Stevens, S., Ouellet-Morin, I., Melhuish, E., & Belsky, J. (2015). Interactive effects of early and recent exposure to stressful contexts on cortisol reactivity in middle childhood. *Journal of Child Psychology and Psychiatry, 56*, 138–146. http://dx.doi.org/10.1111/jcpp.12287

Jedd, K., Hunt, R. H., Cicchetti, D., Hunt, E., Cowell, R. A., Rogosch, F. A., . . . Thomas, K. M. (2015). Long-term consequences of childhood maltreatment: Altered amygdala functional connectivity. *Development and Psychopathology, 27*, 1577–1589. http://dx.doi.org/10.1017/S0954579415000954

Kendall-Tackett, K. (2002). The health effects of childhood abuse: Four pathways by which abuse can influence health. *Child Abuse & Neglect, 26*, 715–729. http://dx.doi.org/10.1016/S0145-2134(02)00343-5

Knudsen, E. I., Heckman, J. J., Cameron, J. L., & Shonkoff, J. P. (2006). Economic, neurobiological, and behavioral perspectives on building America's future workforce. *Proceedings of the National Academy of Sciences of the United States of America, 103,* 10155–10162. http://dx.doi.org/10.1073/pnas.0600888103

Ko, S. J., Ford, J. D., Kassam-Adams, N., Berkowitz, S. J., Wilson, C., Wong, M., . . . Layne, C. M. (2008). Creating trauma-informed systems: Child welfare, education, first responders, health care, juvenile justice. *Professional Psychology: Research and Practice, 39,* 396–404. http://dx.doi.org/10.1037/0735-7028.39.4.396

Kochanska, G. (2001). Emotional development in children with different attachment histories: The first three years. *Child Development, 72,* 474–490. http://dx.doi.org/10.1111/1467-8624.00291

Kuhlman, K. R., Geiss, E. G., Vargas, I., & Lopez-Duran, N. L. (2015). Differential associations between childhood trauma subtypes and adolescent HPA-axis functioning. *Psychoneuroendocrinology, 54,* 103–114. http://dx.doi.org/10.1016/j.psyneuen.2015.01.020

Landreth, G. L. (1983). Play therapy in elementary school settings. In C. E. Schaefer & K. J. O'Connor (Eds.), *Handbook of play therapy* (pp. 200–212). New York, NY: Wiley.

Langevin, R., Hébert, M., & Cossette, L. (2015). Emotion regulation as a mediator of the relation between sexual abuse and behavior problems in preschoolers. *Child Abuse & Neglect, 46,* 16–26. http://dx.doi.org/10.1016/j.chiabu.2015.02.001

Lanier, P., Kohl, P. L., Benz, J., Swinger, D., & Drake, B. (2014). Preventing maltreatment with a community-based implementation of parent–child interaction therapy. *Journal of Child and Family Studies, 23,* 449–460. http://dx.doi.org/10.1007/s10826-012-9708-8

Lansford, J. E., Sharma, C., Malone, P. S., Woodlief, D., Dodge, K. A., Oburu, P., . . . Di Giunta, L. (2014). Corporal punishment, maternal warmth, and child adjustment: A longitudinal study in eight countries. *Journal of Clinical Child and Adolescent Psychology, 43,* 670–685. http://dx.doi.org/10.1080/15374416.2014.893518

LeMoult, J., Chen, M. C., Foland-Ross, L. C., Burley, H. W., & Gotlib, I. H. (2015). Concordance of mother–daughter diurnal cortisol production: Understanding the intergenerational transmission of risk for depression. *Biological Psychology, 108,* 98–104. http://dx.doi.org/10.1016/j.biopsycho.2015.03.019

Leung, C., Tsang, S., Heung, K., & You, I. (1999). Effectiveness of parent–child interaction therapy (PCIT) in Hong Kong. *Research on Social Work Practice, 19,* 304–313. http://dx.doi.org/10.1177/1049731508321713

Lewis, M., & Ghosh Ippen, C. (2004). Rainbow of tears, souls full of hope: Cultural issues related to young children and trauma. In J. D. Osofsky (Ed.), *Young children and trauma: Intervention and treatment* (pp. 11–46). New York, NY: Guilford Press.

Lewis-Morrarty, E., Dozier, M., Bernard, K., Terracciano, S. M., & Moore, S. V. (2012). Cognitive flexibility and theory of mind outcomes among foster children: Preschool follow-up results of a randomized clinical trial. *Journal of Adolescent Health, 51,* S17–S22. http://dx.doi.org/10.1016/j.jadohealth.2012.05.005

Lieberman, A. F. (1990). Culturally sensitive interventions in children and families. *Child and Adolescent Social Work Journal, 7,* 101–120. http://dx.doi.org/10.1007/BF00757648

Lieberman, A. F., Ghosh Ippen, C., & Van Horn, P. (2006). Child–parent psychotherapy: 6-month follow-up of a randomized controlled trial. *Journal of the American Academy of Child & Adolescent Psychiatry, 45,* 913–918. http://dx.doi.org/10.1097/01.chi.0000222784.03735.92

Lieberman, A. F., Ghosh Ippen, C., & Van Horn, P. (2015). *Don't hit my mommy! A manual for child–parent psychotherapy with young children exposed to violence and other trauma* (2nd ed.). Washington, DC: ZERO TO THREE.

Lieberman, A. F., Padron, E., Van Horn, P., & Harris, W. W. (2005). Angels in the nursery: The intergenerational transmission of benevolent parental influences. *Infant Mental Health Journal, 26,* 504–520. http://dx.doi.org/10.1002/imhj.20071

Lieberman, A. F., & Van Horn, P. (2005). *Don't hit my mommy! A manual for child–parent psychotherapy with young witnesses of family violence.* Washington, DC: ZERO TO THREE.

Lieberman, A. F., & Van Horn, P. (2008). *Psychotherapy with infants and young children: Repairing the effects of stress and trauma on early attachment.* New York, NY: Guilford Press.

Lieberman, A. F., Van Horn, P., & Ghosh Ippen, C. (2005). Toward evidence-based treatment: Child-parent psychotherapy with preschoolers exposed to marital violence. *Journal of the American Academy of Child & Adolescent Psychiatry, 44,* 1241–1248. http://dx.doi.org/10.1097/01.chi.0000181047.59702.58

Lieberman, A. F., Weston, D. R., & Pawl, J. H. (1991). Preventive intervention and outcome with anxiously attached dyads. *Child Development, 62,* 199–209. http://dx.doi.org/10.2307/1130715

Lind, T., Bernard, K., Ross, E., & Dozier, M. (2014). Intervention effects on negative affect of CPS-referred children: Results of a randomized clinical trial. *Child Abuse & Neglect, 38,* 1459–1467. http://dx.doi.org/10.1016/j.chiabu.2014.04.004

Luby, J., Belden, A., Botteron, K., Marrus, N., Harms, M. P., Babb, C., . . . Barch, D. (2013, December). The effects of poverty on childhood brain development: The mediating effect of caregiving and stressful life events. *JAMA Pediatrics, 167,* 1135–1142. http://dx.doi.org/10.1001/jamapediatrics.2013.3139

Lupien, S. J., Parent, S., Evans, A. C., Tremblay, R. E., Zelazo, P. D., Corbo, V., . . . Séguin, J. R. (2011). Larger amygdala but no change in hippocampal volume in 10-year-old children exposed to maternal depressive symptomatology since birth. *Proceedings of the National Academy of Sciences of the United States of America, 108*, 14324–14329. http://dx.doi.org/10.1073/pnas.1105371108

Lyons-Ruth, K., & Block, D. (1996). The disturbed caregiving system: Relations among childhood trauma, maternal caregiving, and infant affect and attachment. *Infant Mental Health Journal, 17*, 257–275. http://dx.doi.org/10.1002/(SICI)1097-0355(199623)17:3<257::AID-IMHJ5>3.0.CO;2-L

Masten, A. S., Narayan, A. J., Silverman, W. K., & Osofsky, J. D. (2015). Children in war and disaster. In R. M. Lerner (Ed.), *Handbook of child psychology and developmental science: Vol. 4. Ecological settings and processes in developmental systems* (7th ed., pp. 704–745). New York, NY: Wiley. http://dx.doi.org/10.1002/9781118963418.childpsy418

Masten, A. S., & Osofsky, J. D. (2010). Disasters and their impact on child development: Introduction to the special section. *Child Development, 81*, 1029–1039. http://dx.doi.org/10.1111/j.1467-8624.2010.01452.x

Masten, A. S., & Tellegen, A. (2012). Resilience in developmental psychopathology: Contributions of the Project Competence Longitudinal Study. *Development and Psychopathology, 24*, 345–361. http://dx.doi.org/10.1017/S095457941200003X

Maughan, A., & Cicchetti, D. (2002). Impact of child maltreatment and interadult violence on children's emotion regulation abilities and socioemotional adjustment. *Child Development, 73*, 1525–1542. http://dx.doi.org/10.1111/1467-8624.00488

McCabe, K. M., Yeh, M., Garland, A. F., Lau, A. S., & Chavez, G. (2005). The GANA program: A tailoring approach to adapting parent–child interaction therapy for Mexican Americans. *Education & Treatment of Children, 2*, 111–129.

McCrory, E., De Brito, S. A., & Viding, E. (2010). Research review: The neurobiology and genetics of maltreatment and adversity. *Journal of Child Psychology and Psychiatry, 51*, 1079–1095. http://dx.doi.org/10.1111/j.1469-7610.2010.02271.x

McEwen, B. S., Gray, J. D., & Nasca, C. (2015). Recognizing resilience: Learning from the effects of stress on the brain. *Neurobiology of Stress, 1*, 1–11. http://dx.doi.org/10.1016/j.ynstr.2014.09.001

McEwen, B. S., & Wingfield, J. C. (2003). The concept of allostasis in biology and biomedicine. *Hormones and Behavior, 43*, 2–15. http://dx.doi.org/10.1016/S0018-506X(02)00024-7

McLaughlin, K. A., Sheridan, M. A., Tibu, F., Fox, N. A., Zeanah, C. H., & Nelson, C. A., III. (2015). Causal effects of the early caregiving environment on development of stress response systems in children. *Proceedings of the National*

REFERENCES

Academy of Sciences of the United States of America, 112, 5637–5642. http:// dx.doi.org/10.1073/pnas.1423363112

McNeil, C. B., Eyberg, S. M., Hembree Eisenstadt, T. H., Newcomb, K., & Funderburk, B. (1991). Parent–child interaction therapy with behavior problem children: Generalization of treatment effects to the school setting. *Journal of Clinical Child Psychology, 20*, 140–151. http://dx.doi.org/10.1207/ s15374424jccp2002_5

McNeil, C. B., & Hembree-Kigin, T. L. (2010). *Parent–child interaction therapy.* New York, NY: Springer. http://dx.doi.org/10.1007/978-0-387-88639-8

McNeil, C. B., Herschell, A. D., Gurwitch, R. H., & Clemens-Mowrer, L. (2005). Training foster parents in parent–child interaction therapy. *Education & Treatment of Children, 26*, 182–196.

Meade, E. B., Dozier, M., & Bernard, K. (2014). Using video feedback as a tool in training parent coaches: Promising results from a single-subject design. *Attachment & Human Development, 16*, 356–370. http://dx.doi.org/10.1080/ 14616734.2014.912488

Mehta, M. A., Golembo, N. I., Nosarti, C., Colvert, E., Mota, A., Williams, S. C., . . . Sonuga-Barke, E. J. (2009). Amygdala, hippocampal and corpus callosum size following severe early institutional deprivation: The English and Romanian Adoptees Study pilot. *Journal of Child Psychology and Psychiatry, 50*, 943–951. http://dx.doi.org/10.1111/j.1469-7610.2009.02084.x

Mersky, J. P., Topitzes, J., Janczewski, C. E., & McNeil, C. B. (2015). Enhancing foster parent training with parent–child interaction therapy: Evidence from a randomized field experiment. *Journal of the Society for Social Work and Research, 6*, 591–616. http://dx.doi.org/10.1086/684123

Mikulincer, M., Shaver, P., & Pereg, D. (2003). Attachment theory and affect regulation: The dynamics, development, and cognitive consequences of attachment-related strategies. *Motivation and Emotion, 27*, 77–102. http://dx.doi.org/ 10.1023/A:1024515519160

Miller, F. G. (2009). The randomized controlled trial as a demonstration project: An ethical perspective. *The American Journal of Psychiatry, 166*, 743–745. http://dx.doi.org/10.1176/appi.ajp.2009.09040538

Miller, W. R., & Rollnick, S. (1991). *Motivational interviewing: Preparing people to change addictive behavior.* New York, NY: Guilford Press.

Millum, J., & Emanuel, E. J. (2007, December 21). The ethics of international research with abandoned children. *Science, 318*, 1874–1875. http://dx.doi.org/ 10.1126/science.1153822

National Scientific Council on the Developing Child. (2011). *Building the brain's "air traffic control" system: How early experiences shape the development of executive function.* Retrieved from http://developingchild.harvard.edu/resources/

building-the-brains-air-traffic-control-system-how-early-experiences-shape-the-development-of-executive-function/

National Scientific Council on the Developing Child. (2012). *The science of neglect: The persistent absence of responsive care disrupts the developing brain.* Retrieved from http://developingchild.harvard.edu/resources/the-science-of-neglect-the-persistent-absence-of-responsive-care-disrupts-the-developing-brain/

Nelson, C. A., Fox, N. A., & Zeanah, C. H. (2014). *Romania's abandoned children: Deprivation, brain development and the struggle for recovery.* Cambridge, MA: Harvard University Press. http://dx.doi.org/10.4159/harvard.9780674726079

Nixon, R. D. V., Sweeney, L., Erickson, D. B., & Touyz, S. W. (2003). Parent–child interaction therapy: A comparison of standard and abbreviated treatments for oppositional defiant preschoolers. *Journal of Consulting and Clinical Psychology, 71*, 251–260. http://dx.doi.org/10.1037/0022-006X.71.2.251

Ondersma, S. J. (2002). Predictors of neglect within low-SES families: The importance of substance abuse. *American Journal of Orthopsychiatry, 72*, 383–391. http://dx.doi.org/10.1037/0002-9432.72.3.383

Osofsky, J. D. (1995). The effects of exposure to violence on young children. *American Psychologist, 50*, 782–788. http://dx.doi.org/10.1037/0003-066X.50.9.782

Osofsky, J. D. (2011). *Clinical work with traumatized young children.* New York, NY: Guilford Press.

Osofsky, J. D. (2016). Infant mental health. In J. Norcross, M. Domenech-Rodriguez, & D. Freedheim (Eds.), *APA handbook of clinical psychology* (pp. 43–58). Washington, DC: American Psychological Association.

Osofsky, J. D., Cohen, G., & Drell, M. (1995). The effects of trauma on young children: A case of 2-year-old twins. *The International Journal of Psychoanalysis, 76*, 595–607.

Osofsky, J. D., Drell, M. J., Osofsky, H. J., Hansel, T. C., & Williams, A. (2016). Infant mental health training for child and adolescent psychiatry: A comprehensive model. *Academic Psychiatry.* Advance online publication. http://dx.doi.org/10.1007/s40596-016-0609-9

Osofsky, J. D., & Lieberman, A. F. (2011). A call for integrating a mental health perspective into systems of care for abused and neglected infants and young children. *American Psychologist, 66*, 120–128. http://dx.doi.org/10.1037/a0021630

Osofsky, J. D., & Weatherston, D. J. (Eds.). (2016). Advances in reflective supervision and consultation: Pushing boundaries and integrating new ideas into training and practice [Special issue]. *Infant Mental Health Journal, 37.*

Pat-Horenczyk, R., Cohen, S., Ziv, Y., Achituv, M., Asulin-Peretz, L., Blanchard, T. R., . . . Brom, D. (2015). Emotion regulation in mothers and young children faced with trauma. *Infant Mental Health Journal, 36*, 337–348. http://dx.doi. org/10.1002/imhj.21515

Patterson, G. R. (1982). *Coercive family process.* Eugene, OR: Castalia.

Pears, K. C., & Capaldi, D. M. (2001). Intergenerational transmission of abuse: A two-generational prospective study of an at-risk sample. *Child Abuse & Neglect, 25*, 1439–1461. http://dx.doi.org/10.1016/S0145-2134(01)00286-1

Pechtel, P., & Pizzagalli, D. A. (2011). Effects of early life stress on cognitive and affective function: An integrated review of human literature. *Psychopharmacology, 214*, 55–70. http://dx.doi.org/10.1007/s00213-010-2009-2

Perry, B. D., & Pollard, R. (1997, October). *Altered brain development following global neglect.* Paper presented at the meeting of the Society for Neuroscience, New Orleans, LA.

Rhoades, B. L., Greenberg, M. T., Lanza, S. T., & Blair, C. (2011). Demographic and familial predictors of early executive function development: Contribution of a person-centered perspective. *Journal of Experimental Child Psychology, 108*, 638–662. http://dx.doi.org/10.1016/j.jecp.2010.08.004

Rid, A. (2012). When is research socially valuable? Lessons from the Bucharest Early Intervention Project: Commentary on a case study in the ethics of mental health research. *Journal of Nervous and Mental Disease, 200*, 248–249. http://dx.doi.org/10.1097/NMD.0b013e318247d124

Rifkin-Graboi, A., Kong, L., Sim, L. W., Sanmugam, S., Broekman, B. F. P., Chen, H., . . . Qiu, A. (2015). Maternal sensitivity, infant limbic structure volume and functional connectivity: A preliminary study. *Translational Psychiatry, 5*, e668. http://dx.doi.org/10.1038/tp.2015.133

Roben, C. K. P., Dozier, M., Caron, E. B., & Bernard, K. (in press). Moving an evidence-based parenting program into the community. *Child Development.*

Roberts, A. L., Chen, Y., Slopen, N., McLaughlin, K. A., Koenen, K. C., & Austin, S. B. (2015). Maternal experience of abuse in childhood and depressive symptoms in adolescent and adult offspring: A 21-year longitudinal study. *Depression and Anxiety, 32*, 709–719. http://dx.doi.org/10.1002/da.22395

Schuhmann, E. M., Foote, R. C., Eyberg, S. M., Boggs, S. R., & Algina, J. (1998). Efficacy of parent–child interaction therapy: Interim report of a randomized trial with short-term maintenance. *Journal of Clinical Child Psychology, 27*, 34–45. http://dx.doi.org/10.1207/s15374424jccp2701_4

Shalev, I., Entringer, S., Wadhwa, P. D., Wolkowitz, O. M., Puterman, E., Lin, J., & Epel, E. S. (2013). Stress and telomere biology: A lifespan perspective. *Psychoneuroendocrinology, 38*, 1835–1842. http://dx.doi.org/10.1016/j.psyneuen. 2013.03.010

Shonkoff, J. P., Garner, A. S., Committee on Psychosocial Aspects of Child and Family Health, Committee on Early Childhood, Adoption, and Dependent

Care, Section on Developmental and Behavioral Pediatrics, Siegel, B. S., . . . Wood, D. L. (2012). The lifelong effects of early childhood adversity and toxic stress. *Pediatrics, 129,* e232–e246. http://dx.doi.org/10.1542/peds.2011-2663

Snyder, H. N. (2000). *Sexual assault of young children as reported to law enforcement: Victim, incident, and offender characteristics.* Retrieved from https://www.bjs.gov/content/pub/pdf/saycrle.pdf

Solomon, M., Ono, M., Timmer, S., & Goodlin-Jones, B. (2008). The effectiveness of parent–child interaction therapy for families of children on the autism spectrum. *Journal of Autism and Developmental Disorders, 38,* 1767–1776. http://dx.doi.org/10.1007/s10803-008-0567-5

Stoltenborgh, M., Bakermans-Kranenburg, M. J., Alink, L. R. A., & van IJzendoorn, M. H. (2012). The universality of childhood emotional abuse: A meta-analysis of worldwide prevalence. *Journal of Aggression, Maltreatment & Trauma, 21,* 870–890. http://dx.doi.org/10.1080/10926771.2012.708014

Stoltenborgh, M., Bakermans-Kranenburg, M. J., & van IJzendoorn, M. H. (2013). The neglect of child neglect: A meta-analytic review of the prevalence of neglect. *Social Psychiatry and Psychiatric Epidemiology, 48,* 345–355. http://dx.doi.org/10.1007/s00127-012-0549-y

Stovall, K. C., & Dozier, M. (2000). The development of attachment in new relationships: Single subject analyses for 10 foster infants. *Development and Psychopathology, 12,* 133–156. http://dx.doi.org/10.1017/S0954579400002029

Stronach, E. P., Toth, S. L., Rogosch, F., & Cicchetti, D. (2013). Preventive interventions and sustained attachment security in maltreated children. *Development and Psychopathology, 25,* 919–930. http://dx.doi.org/10.1017/S0954579413000278

Teicher, M. H., & Samson, J. A. (2016). Annual research review: Enduring neurobiological effects of childhood abuse and neglect. *Journal of Child Psychology and Psychiatry, 57,* 241–266. http://dx.doi.org/10.1111/jcpp.12507

Thomas, R., & Zimmer-Gembeck, M. J. (2011). Accumulating evidence for parent–child interaction therapy in the prevention of child maltreatment. *Child Development, 82,* 177–192. http://dx.doi.org/10.1111/j.1467-8624.2010.01548.x

Thomas, R., & Zimmer-Gembeck, M. J. (2012). Parent–child interaction therapy: An evidence-based treatment for child maltreatment. *Child Maltreatment, 17,* 253–266. http://dx.doi.org/10.1177/1077559512459555

Timmer, S. G., Urquiza, A. J., & Zebell, N. (2006). Challenging foster caregiver-maltreated child relationships: The effectiveness of parent–child interaction therapy. *Children and Youth Services Review, 28,* 1–19. http://dx.doi.org/10.1016/j.childyouth.2005.01.006

Timmer, S. G., Urquiza, A. J., Zebell, N. M., & McGrath, J. M. (2005). Parent–child interaction therapy: Application to maltreating parent–child dyads. *Child Abuse & Neglect, 29,* 825–842. http://dx.doi.org/10.1016/j.chiabu.2005.01.003

Timmer, S. G., Ware, L. M., Urquiza, A. J., & Zebell, N. M. (2010). The effectiveness of parent–child interaction therapy for victims of interparental violence. *Violence and Victims, 25,* 486–503. http://dx.doi.org/10.1891/0886-6708.25.4.486

Toth, S. L., & Cicchetti, D. (2013). A developmental psychopathology perspective on child maltreatment. *Child Maltreatment, 18,* 135–139. http://dx.doi.org/10.1177/1077559513500380

Toth, S. L., Maughan, A., Manly, J. T., Spagnola, M., & Cicchetti, D. (2002). The relative efficacy of two interventions in altering maltreated preschool children's representational models: Implications for attachment theory. *Development and Psychopathology, 14,* 877–908. http://dx.doi.org/10.1017/S095457940200411X

Toth, S. L., Rogosch, F. A., Manly, J. T., & Cicchetti, D. (2006). The efficacy of toddler–parent psychotherapy to reorganize attachment in the young offspring of mothers with major depressive disorder: A randomized preventive trial. *Journal of Consulting and Clinical Psychology, 74,* 1006–1016. http://dx.doi.org/10.1037/0022-006X.74.6.1006

Tottenham, N., Hare, T. A., Quinn, B. T., McCarry, T. W., Nurse, M., Gilhooly, T., . . . Casey, B. J. (2010). Prolonged institutional rearing is associated with atypically large amygdala volume and difficulties in emotion regulation. *Developmental Science, 13,* 46–61. http://dx.doi.org/10.1111/j.1467-7687.2009.00852.x

Tronick, E., Als, H., Adamson, L., Wise, S., & Brazelton, B. (1978). The infant's response to entrapment between contradictory messages in face-to-face interaction. *Journal of the American Academy of Child Psychiatry, 17,* 1–13. http://dx.doi.org/10.1016/S0002-7138(09)62273-1

Tronick, E., & Beeghly, M. (2011). Infants' meaning-making and the development of mental health problems. *American Psychologist, 66,* 107–119. http://dx.doi.org/10.1037/a0021631

UC Davis Children's Hospital. (2016). *PCIT web course.* Retrieved from http://pcit.ucdavis.edu/pcit-web-course/

Urquiza, A. J., & McNeil, C. B. (1996). Parent–child interaction therapy: An intensive dyadic intervention for physically abusive families. *Child Maltreatment, 1,* 134–144. http://dx.doi.org/10.1177/1077559596001002005

Urquiza, A. J., & Timmer, S. G. (2014). Parent–child interaction therapy for maltreated children. In S. G. Timmer & A. J. Urquiza (Eds.), *Evidence-based approaches for the treatment of maltreated children* (pp. 123–144). New York, NY: Springer. http://dx.doi.org/10.1007/978-94-007-7404-9_8

U.S. Department of Health and Human Services, Administration for Children and Families, Administration on Children, Youth and Families, Children's Bureau. (2015). *Child maltreatment 2013*. Retrieved from http://www.acf.hhs.gov/programs/cb/research-data-technology/statistics-research/child-maltreatment

Vachon, D. D., Krueger, R. F., Rogosch, F. A., & Cicchetti, D. (2015, November). Assessment of the harmful psychiatric and behavioral effects of different forms of child maltreatment. *JAMA Psychiatry, 72*, 1135–1142. http://dx.doi.org/10.1001/jamapsychiatry.2015.1792

Van den Bergh, B. R. H. (2011). Developmental programming of early brain and behaviour development and mental health: A conceptual framework. *Developmental Medicine and Child Neurology, 53*, 19–23. http://dx.doi.org/10.1111/j.1469-8749.2011.04057.x

van IJzendoorn, M. H. (1995). Adult attachment representations, parental responsiveness, and infant attachment: A meta-analysis on the predictive validity of the Adult Attachment Interview. *Psychological Bulletin, 117*, 387–403. http://dx.doi.org/10.1037/0033-2909.117.3.387

van IJzendoorn, M. H., Schuengel, C., & Bakermans-Kranenburg, M. J. (1999). Disorganized attachment in early childhood: Meta-analysis of precursors, concomitants, and sequelae. *Development and Psychopathology, 11*, 225–250. http://dx.doi.org/10.1017/S0954579499002035

Votruba-Drzal, E., Miller, P., & Coley, R. L. (2016). Poverty, urbanicity, and children's development of early academic skills. *Child Development Perspectives, 10*, 3–9. http://dx.doi.org/10.1111/cdep.12152

Wagner, S. (2010). Research on PCIT. In C. B. McNeil & T. L. Hembree-Kigin (Eds.), *Parent–child interaction therapy* (pp. 17–29). New York, NY: Springer.

Ware, L., & Herschell, A. (2010). Child physical abuse. In C. B. McNeil & T. L. Hembree-Kigin (Eds.), *Parent–child interaction therapy* (pp. 255–284). New York, NY: Springer.

Waters, S. F., West, T. V., & Mendes, W. B. (2014). Stress contagion: Physiological covariation between mothers and infants. *Psychological Science, 25*, 934–942. http://dx.doi.org/10.1177/0956797613518352

Weems, C. F., & Carrion, V. G. (2007). The association between PTSD symptoms and salivary cortisol in youth: The role of time since the trauma. *Journal of Traumatic Stress, 20*, 903–907. http://dx.doi.org/10.1002/jts.20251

Welsh, J. A., Nix, R. L., Blair, C., Bierman, K. L., & Nelson, K. E. (2010). The development of cognitive skills and gains in academic school readiness for children from low-income families. *Journal of Educational Psychology, 102*, 43–53. http://dx.doi.org/10.1037/a0016738

Widom, C. S. (1989). Does violence beget violence? A critical examination of the literature. *Psychological Bulletin, 106*, 3–28. http://dx.doi.org/10.1037/0033-2909.106.1.3

Wilson, S. R., Rack, J. J., Shi, X., & Norris, A. M. (2008). Comparing physically abusive, neglectful, and non-maltreating parents during interactions with their children: A meta-analysis of observational studies. *Child Abuse & Neglect, 32*, 897–911. http://dx.doi.org/10.1016/j.chiabu.2008.01.003

Zeanah, C. H., Fox, N. A., & Nelson, C. A. (2012). The Bucharest Early Intervention Project: Case study in the ethics of mental health research. *Journal of Nervous and Mental Disease, 200*, 243–247. http://dx.doi.org/10.1097/NMD.0b013e318247d275

ZERO TO THREE. (2005). *DC: 0–3R: Diagnostic classification of mental health and developmental disorders of infancy and early childhood* (Rev.). Washington, DC: Author.

ZERO TO THREE. (2012). *Frequently asked questions about brain development.* Retrieved from https://www.zerotothree.org/resources/series/frequently-asked-questions-about-brain-development

Index

Abandonment, 91
ABC intervention. *See* Attachment and biobehavioral catch-up intervention
Abuse. *See specific headings*
Academic achievement, 115
ACE (Adverse Childhood Experiences) Study, 3–4, 8–9
Active ignoring, 82
ADHD (attention-deficit/ hyperactivity disorder), 21, 75
Adolescence, 8
Adoption, 75
Adoption and Safe Families Act, 100
Adult-focused goals (child–parent psychotherapy), 45
Adverse Childhood Experiences (ACE) Study, 3–4, 8–9
Affect regulation
    and attachment and biobehavioral catch-up intervention, 73
    in child–parent psychotherapy, 42, 46
African Americans
    child–parent psychotherapy with, 42
    parent–child interaction therapy with, 77

Age of child, 97
Aggression
    childhood, 55–56
    and parent–child interaction therapy, 89
    parent–child interaction therapy for, 75
Ainsworth, M. D. S., 36
Allostatic overload, 21
Amygdala, 21, 23–25
Anger, 43, 73
ANS (autonomic nervous system), 20–23
Anxiety, 21, 24, 77
Arousal, 48, 64, 92
Asian populations
    child–parent psychotherapy with, 42
    parent–child interaction therapy with, 77
Assessment
    for attachment and biobehavioral catch-up intervention, 67
    in child–parent psychotherapy, 44–46, 48–49
    and observations, 111
    in parent–child interaction therapy, 88–89

Attachment. *See also* Attachment
  and biobehavioral catch-up
  intervention
  and child–parent psychotherapy,
    41–43, 46
  overview of trauma's impact on,
    36–38
  and socioemotional development,
    116
  as theoretical framework, 95–96
Attachment and biobehavioral
    catch-up (ABC) intervention,
    61–74
  assessment for, 67
  components of, 94–96
  and criterion in treatment
    selection, 97–101
  design of, 65–66
  development of, 61
  evidence base for, 61, 72–73
  fidelity to, 66–67
  session-by-session overview of,
    67–71
  targets of, 62–65
  therapeutic action of, 93
  training manual for, 95
Attentional control, 27
Attention-deficit/hyperactivity
    disorder (ADHD), 21, 75
Autism spectrum disorder, 77
Automatic behaviors, 70–71
Autonomic nervous system (ANS),
    20–23
Autonomy, child, 63
Avoidance, 43, 48, 92
Avoidant attachment style, 37

Baumrind, D., 76
Behavioral functioning, 46, 50–51
Behavior management, 75
BEIP (Bucharest Early Intervention
    Project), 22
Bernard, K., 23, 63, 64, 72, 73

Bias, therapist, 96
Biological development, 115
Biological reactivity and regulation,
    20–25
Biological rhythms, 54
Biological sensitivity to context, 21–22
Biological stress response systems, 8
Blair, C., 30
Blehar, M. C., 36
Blood, E. A., 31
Borrego, J., Jr., 86
Bosquet Enlow, M., 23, 31, 34
Brain abnormalities, 8
Brain development, 20–27, 115
Briggs-Gowan, M. J., 3
"Broaden-and-build" cycle, 20
Bucharest Early Intervention Project
    (BEIP), 22
Bullying, 9

Caregiving
  and brain development, 25
  pathogenic vs. sensitive, 98
  suboptimal, 28–30
Caron, E. B., 67
CDI (child-directed interaction),
    81–83, 86, 87
Cellular aging, 26–27
Center for the Developing Child
    (Harvard University), 111
Center for Youth Wellness, 9
Chase, R. M., 77
Child Behavior Checklist–
    Dysregulation Profile, 34
Child-directed interaction (CDI),
    81–83, 86, 87
Child-focused goals (child–parent
    psychotherapy), 45
Childhood exposure to trauma, 3–10
  cumulative experiences of, 8–10
  and importance of parent–child
    relationship, 6–8
  prevalence of, 3–4

and research on polyvictimization,
10
symptoms associated with, 4–5
and trauma-informed systems, 5–6
Child neglect. *See also* Maltreatment
developmental effects of, 115
and parent–child interaction
therapy, 92
Child–parent psychotherapy (CPP),
41–59
and attachment and biobehavioral
catch-up intervention, 62
components of, 94–96
core interventions of, 52–58
course of, 44–45
and criterion in treatment
selection, 97–101
evidence base for, 43–44
foundations of, 47
other therapeutic interventions vs.,
47–48
phases of, 48–52
reflective supervision in, 58
therapeutic action of, 93
training manual for, 95
treatment planning for, 46
Child Protective Services (CPS), 16,
18, 72
Child welfare system, 7
Cicchetti, D., 31, 35, 36, 44
Clinical training, 95, 113
Coercion theory, 76, 84
Cognitive development, 27–32, 115
Cognitive flexibility, 27, 73
Cognitive functioning, 46
Cohen, D. J., 32
Community agencies, 61
Community standard treatment, 43
Complex trauma, 100
Conduct behaviors, 75
Content fidelity, 58
Co-regulation, 34
Corporal punishment, 19

Cowell, R. A., 31
CPP. *See* Child–parent psychotherapy
CPS (Child Protective Services), 16,
18, 72
Culturally-appropriate treatments, 6
Cultural values, 42, 96
Cumulative traumatic experiences,
8–10

Deaths, 91
Depression, 21, 26, 49
Description (parent–child interaction
therapy), 82
Developmental expectations, 42
Developmental impact of trauma,
15–39
on brain and physiology, 20–27
on cognitive and linguistic
development, 27–32
on socioemotional development,
32–38
and treatment selection, 98
and types of trauma exposure,
16–20
DHHS (U.S. Department of Health
and Human Services), 16, 19
Differential susceptibility, 21–22
Discipline beliefs, 42, 90
Disorganized attachment style, 37, 62
Disruptive behavior, 98
Divorce, 75
DNA methylation, 27
Domestic violence
in ACE Study, 9
and cognitive development, 31–32
negative outcomes in households
with, 8
overview, 19–20
and parent–child interaction
therapy, 76
parent–child interaction therapy for
children exposed to, 86–87
trauma of, 7

"DON'T" behavior, 82
Dozier, Mary, 23, 61, 63, 65, 70–73
Dyadic Parent–Child Interaction
    Coding System–IV
    (DPICS-IV), 79
Dyadic relational fidelity, 57
Dyadic treatments. *See specific
    interventions*

Early Catastrophe, The (B. B. Hart &
    T. R. Risley), 28
ECBI (Eyberg Child Behavior
    Inventory), 78
Egeland, B., 31
Eigsti, I. M., 31
Emotional abuse
    in ACE Study, 9
    research on impact of, 18
Emotional functioning, 46, 50–51
Emotional neglect, 9
Emotional process fidelity, 57
Emotion regulation, 5, 33–36, 116
Emotions, reading of, 71
Engagement, therapy, 48–49
Ensor, R., 29, 30
Enthusiasm, 82
Epigenetic programming, 26
Essex, M. J., 27
Evidence-based assessment
        and treatment
    and attachment and biobehavioral
        catch-up intervention, 61,
        72–73
    benefits of, 110–111
    and child–parent psychotherapy,
        43–44
    culturally appropriate, 6
    dissemination of, 112
    and parent–child interaction
        therapy, 75, 77
Executive functioning, 27
Exercise, 8
Externalizing problems, 75

Eyberg, S. M., 76, 77
Eyberg Child Behavior Inventory
    (ECBI), 78

Familial risk factors, 28–30, 115
Feedback (parent–child interaction
    therapy), 80
Fernald, A., 29
Fidelity
    to attachment and biobehavioral
        catch-up intervention,
        66–67
    to child–parent psychotherapy
        model, 56–58
Finkelhor, D., 10
Foster care
    in ACE Study, 9
    longitudinal studies of children
        raised in, 22
    parent–child interaction therapy
        for children in, 76, 87, 92
    and treatment selection, 100
Frightening behavior, 64, 67, 70, 89

Gee, D. G., 24
Gene expression, 26–27, 115
Ghosh Ippen, C., 44
Glucocorticoid receptors, 25
Greenberg, M. T., 30
Groves, B. M., 32

Hanf, C., 76
Harris Center for Infant Mental
    Health, 4
Hart, B. B., 28, 31
A Hidden Crisis (report), 9
Hippocampus, 25
Home-based interventions, 96
Hostinar, C. E., 73
HPA (hypothalamic–pituitary–
    adrenal) axis, 20–23, 64–65
Hughes, C., 29, 30
Hyperarousal, 92

Hypervigilance, 48
Hypothalamic–pituitary–adrenal
    (HPA) axis, 20–23, 64–65

Ignoring, active, 82
Imitation, 82
Incarcerated individuals, 9
Inhibitory control, 27
Insecure attachment style, 36
Institutionalization, 26
Intake interviews, 78
Intellectual impairments, 77
Intelligence quotient (IQ), 31–32,
    115
Intergenerational trauma, 100
Internalizing problems, 75
Interpersonal trauma, 10
Interventions. See Treatment selection;
    specific interventions
In-the-moment coaching, 65–66
Intrusiveness, 64, 68–70
In vivo parent coaching, 75
IQ (intelligence quotient), 31–32,
    115
Irving Harris Foundation, 4

Kaiser Permanente, 8
Kendall-Tackett, K., 38
King, L., 23
Kochanska, G., 36

Language development, 27–32, 115
Lanier, P., 85, 87
Lanza, S. T., 30
Latinos
    child–parent psychotherapy with,
        42
    parent–child interaction therapy
        with, 77
Lieberman, A. F., 44
"Limbic scars," 25
Lind, T., 72
Linguistic development, 27–32, 115

Longitudinal research designs, 31
Loss histories, 91
Louisiana State University Health
    Sciences Center (LSUHSC), 110
Luby, J., 25

MacArthur Story Stem Battery, 43
Maltreatment
    and brain development, 25
    and cognitive development, 31
    defined, 16
    overview, 16–19
Managed care, 99
Marans, S., 32
Marchman, V. A., 29
Maternal depression, 26
Maughan, A., 35, 36
McLaughlin, K. A., 22
McNeil, C. B., 85–87
Meade, E. B., 63, 66
Medical issues, 98
Memory, 27
Mental Health and Substance Abuse
    Services Administration, 43
Mental illness
    in ACE Study, 9
    and child–parent psychotherapy,
        46
    and emotion regulation, 35
    negative outcomes in households
        with, 8
Miller, W. R., 85
Minnesota Longitudinal Study of
    Parents and Children, 31
Modeling, 47
Motivational interviewing, 85

National Child Traumatic Stress
    Network (NCTSN), 6, 111
Neural circuitry, 21
Neural coupling, 24–25
Neurobiological effects of trauma, 8
Neurological issues, 98

New Orleans Police Department,
110–111
Nondirective play therapy, 75
Nurturance, 63, 64, 68–69, 71

Oppositional defiant disorder, 77
Orphanages, 22
Osofsky, Joy D., 4, 109
Overeating, 8

Parental insensitivity, 98
Parent–child interaction therapy
(PCIT), 75–92
adaptations of, 75–76
and application to trauma-exposed
children, 83–88
assessment in, 88–89
child-directed interaction in,
89–90
components of, 94–96
and criterion in treatment
selection, 97–101
evidence base for, 75, 77
parent-directed interaction in, 90
stages of, 78–83
termination in, 90–91
therapeutic action of, 93
training manual for, 95
Parent–child relationship
attachment in, 36–38
importance of, 6–8
Parent-directed interaction (PDI), 81,
83, 86, 87, 90
Parenting goals, 42
Parenting styles, 76–77
Pat-Horenczyk, R., 34
Patterson, G. R., 76, 84
PCIT. See Parent–child interaction
therapy
PDI (parent-directed interaction), 81,
83, 86, 87, 90
Physical abuse, 9, 84–86, 92
Physical neglect, 9

Physical safety, 46
Physiology, 20–27
Play
in child–parent psychotherapy,
48, 54
importance of, 5
in parent–child interaction
therapy, 76–77, 79, 89–90
repetitive, 48
and touch, 71
Policy, 112–113
Polyvictimization, 10–11
Ports of entry, 50, 52–54
Positive parental presence, 23
Posttraumatic stress disorder (PTSD)
and biological dysregulation, 21
child–parent psychotherapy for
treatment of, 44
and disorganized attachment, 37
mothers with, 34
and parent–child interaction
therapy, 92
and treatment selection, 98
in young children, 4
Poverty, 3, 29, 96
Praise, 82
Prefrontal cortex, 21, 23–25
Prevention of childhood trauma,
112–113
PRIDE skills (parent–child interaction
therapy), 82
Procedural coding, 99
Procedural fidelity, 57
Promiscuity, 8
Protective factors, 6
Proximity seeking, 36
Psychobiological regulation, 62, 64–65
Psychodynamic framework, 95–96
Psychoeducational home visitation, 43
Psychological safety, 46
PTSD. See Posttraumatic stress disorder
Public policy, 112–113
Punishments, 90

Racism, 9
Reassessment (child–parent psychotherapy), 46
Recidivism, 85
Reciprocity, 46, 50
Re-experiencing (posttraumatic symptom), 92
Referrals, 99–100
Reflection (parent–child interaction therapy), 82
Reflective guidance (therapeutic intervention), 53
Reflective practice fidelity, 56–57
Reflective supervision, 58
Relationship-based therapy, 7
Relationship goals (child–parent psychotherapy), 45
Repetitive play, 48
Resilience, 6, 20
Resistance, 43
Resistant attachment style, 37
Rhoades, B. L., 30
Rifkin-Graboi, A., 25
Risley, T. R., 28, 31
Roberts, A. L., 35
Rogosch, F. A., 31, 44
Rollnick, S., 85

Safe Babies Court Teams (SBCTs), 110
Safety
    in child–parent psychotherapy, 42, 45, 46, 52
    physical, 46
    and physical touch, 71
    psychological, 46
Samson, J. A., 25–26
Scaffolding, 29–30
Screening for trauma
    importance of, 9
    overview, 6
Secure attachment, 63
Self-blame, 19
Self-motivational enhancement module, 85–86

Sensory integration, 54
Separation anxiety disorder, 24, 77
SES (socioeconomic status), 29, 96
Severe mental illness, 100
Sexual abuse
    in ACE Study, 9
    and maltreatment, 19
    and parent–child interaction therapy, 92
    and treatment selection, 100
Shame, 19
Simons, R., 72
Smoking, 8
Social learning theory, 76, 95–96
Socioeconomic status (SES), 29, 96
Socioemotional development, 32–38, 116
"Speaking for baby" (therapeutic intervention), 53, 111
Still Face Paradigm, 34
Stronach, E. P., 44
Sturge-Apple, M. L., 44
Substance abuse
    in ACE Study, 9
    by adolescents, 8
    and child–parent psychotherapy, 46
    negative outcomes in households with, 8
Supervision, 58, 66–67
Susceptibility, differential, 21–22
Sutter-Eyberg Student Behavior Inventory–Revised, 78
Symptoms
    clinical emphasis on, 112
    trauma-related, 48
Synchrony, 63–64, 68, 69, 71

Teicher, M. H., 25–26
Telomeres, 26
Termination
    in child–parent psychotherapy, 56
    in parent–child interaction therapy, 90–91

Theoretical frameworks, 95–96
Theory of mind, 73
Thomas, R., 86, 87, 91
Timmer, S. G., 89
Toth, S. L., 31, 44
Touch, physical, 71
Training, clinical, 95, 113
Trauma
    childhood exposure to. *See*
        Childhood exposure to
        trauma
    complex, 100
    intergenerational, 100
    interpersonal, 10
    neurobiological effects of, 8
Trauma framework fidelity, 57
Trauma-informed practice, 5–6
    development of, 9
    guidelines for, 6
Trauma narratives, 46, 51–52
Traumatic Events Screening
        Inventory–Parent Reported
        Revised, 49
Treatment planning, 46
Treatment selection, 93–108
    case illustrations, 100–108
    and comparison of treatments,
        94–96
    considerations in, 96–97
    criterion in, 97–100
Trust
    in child–parent psychotherapy, 42,
        45, 52
    and cultural considerations, 96

Unsafe neighborhoods, 9
Urquiza, A. J., 85, 86, 89
U.S. Department of Health and
        Human Services (DHHS),
        16, 19
U.S. Department of Justice, 19

Van Horn, P., 44
Videos, 66, 70, 82
Violence
    in ACE Study, 9
    developmental effects of, 115
    domestic. *See* Domestic violence
Violence Intervention Program,
        110–111

WAIMH (World Association
        for Infant Mental Health),
        109–110
Wall, S., 36
Waters, E., 36
Weisleder, A., 29
Working memory, 27
World Association for Infant Mental
        Health (WAIMH), 109–110
Wright, R. J., 31
Wright, R. O., 31

ZERO TO THREE: National Center
        for Infants, Toddlers and
        Families (ZTT), 110
Zimmer-Gembeck, M. J., 86, 87, 91
Zuckerman, B., 32
Zwerling, J., 23

About the Authors

Joy D. Osofsky, PhD, Paul J. Ramsay Chair of Psychiatry and a professor of Pediatrics and Psychiatry at Louisiana State University Health Sciences Center (LSUHSC) in New Orleans, is both a clinical and developmental psychologist. She is director of the LSUHSC Harris Center for Infant Mental Health. Among her scholarly achievements, Dr. Osofsky has written or edited nine books, including the *Handbook of Infant Development* and *Clinical Work With Traumatized Young Children,* and is coeditor of the *WAIMH Handbook of Infant Mental Health.* Dr. Osofsky is past president of ZERO TO THREE: National Center for Infants, Toddlers and Families and the World Association for Infant Mental Health. In 2016, she wrote the first chapter on infant mental health in the *Handbook of Clinical Psychology.* She has played a leadership role in the Gulf Region in developing response and recovery efforts following Hurricane Katrina and the Deepwater Horizon oil spill. In 2007, Dr. Osofsky received the Sarah Haley Memorial Award for Clinical Excellence from the International Society for Traumatic Stress Studies, for trauma work. In 2010, she was honored with a Presidential Commendation from the American Psychiatric Association for her work in the aftermath of Hurricane Katrina. Dr. Osofsky was recognized with the 2014 Reginald Lourie Award for leadership in the field of infant mental health and outstanding contributions to the health and welfare of children and families. She does research, intervention, and clinical work with infants, children, and families exposed to community and domestic violence, maltreatment, trauma, and disasters and is the clinical consultant for Safe Babies Court Teams for ZERO TO THREE. Dr. Osofsky is currently the coprincipal investigator for the Terrorism and Disaster Coalition for Child and Family Resilience, a National Child Traumatic Stress Network Center initiative funded by the Substance Abuse and Mental Health Services Administration. She serves a key role in helping state and national legislators and policymakers understand the behavioral health needs of children, especially young children.

Phillip T. Stepka, PsyD, is an assistant professor of clinical psychiatry at LSUHSC, where he serves as a member of the teaching faculty for the Harris Center for Infant Mental Health. His interests include trauma throughout the lifespan, child maltreatment, infant mental health, fetal alcohol effects and syndrome, pervasive developmental disorders, sexual abuse and sexual behavior problems, and risk and resiliency factors in military families. Dr. Stepka serves as project coordinator for the LSUHSC site for the Substance Abuse and Mental Health Services Administration–funded Early Trauma Treatment Network, a center in the National Child Traumatic Stress Network. He is a child–parent psychotherapy national trainer and consults on adaptations of other evidence-based practices for young children across the country. Dr. Stepka provides evaluative, therapeutic, and consultation services to military children, their families, and educators at the Belle Chasse Naval Air Station/Joint Reserve Base in South Louisiana. He also collaborates with the military's Family Advocacy Program in developing and implementing resilience-building interventions for young children with deployed caregivers and providing multidisciplinary treatment to military families affected by abuse, neglect, and domestic violence.

Lucy S. King, BA, is currently a PhD student in the Department of Psychology at Stanford University, where she studies the impact of environmental adversity on psychobiological development from the first months of life through adolescence. Her areas of interest include novel methods for measuring positive and negative aspects of the early environment and the effects of caregiving behavior on the development of stress response systems. She has previously held research positions in the Department of Psychiatry at Boston Children's Hospital and at Louisiana State University Health Sciences Center. Ms. King has published and presented peer-reviewed research clarifying the associations between caregiving, early stress exposure, and biological reactivity and regulation in infancy and childhood. She has also conducted research on developmental psychopathology in children and adolescents exposed to natural and technological disasters. She is the recipient of a Graduate Research Fellowship from the National Science Foundation.